THE BEST OF WINDSOR COOKBOOK

The Best of
Windsor
Cookbook

JONATHAN PINTO

with photographs by Mauro Chechi

BIBLIOASIS
WINDSOR, ONTARIO

Introductions Copyright © Jonathan Pinto, 2016
Photographs Copyright © Mauro Chechi, 2016
Individual recipes copyright to each contributing restaurant. Used with permission by Biblioasis.

All rights reserved. No part of this publication may be reproduced or transmitted in any form or by any means, electronic or mechanical, including photocopying, recording, or any information storage and retrieval system, without permission in writing from the publisher or a licence from The Canadian Copyright Licensing Agency (Access Copyright). For an Access Copyright licence, visit www.accesscopyright.ca or call toll-free to 1-800-893-5777.

FIRST EDITION

Library and Archives Canada Cataloguing in Publication

Pinto, Jonathan, author
    The best of Windsor cookbook / Jonathan Pinto.

Issued in print and electronic formats.
ISBN 978-1-77196-137-0 (paperback).--ISBN 978-1-77196-138-7 (ebook)

    1. Cooking. 2. Cooking--Ontario--Windsor. 3. Cookbooks. I. Title.

TX714.P567 2016   641.509713'32   C2016-901868-7
                                                     C2016-901869-5

Readied for the press by Daniel Wells and Chris Andrechek
Photographs by Mauro Chechi
Typeset and designed by Chris Andrechek

Published with the generous assistance of the Department of Canadian Heritage.

 Canadian   Patrimoine
Heritage   canadien

PRINTED AND BOUND IN CANADA

Restaurants and chefs often come and go, and menus are ever changing. We recommend you call ahead to obtain current information before visiting any of the establishments in this book.

Contents

Introduction

"YOU'RE MOVING WHERE?!"

I heard these words more than once, often combined with a wrinkled nose, when I told friends and family that I was moving to the edge of the province to work for CBC's morning radio program in Windsor.

I didn't know what the fuss was about. Growing up in Peterborough, a small university town about 90 minutes northeast of Toronto, Windsor wasn't really on my radar. I knew about its ties with the auto industry, and that it was close to the border. Some distant relatives had lived there once, while working in Michigan's health-care sector, but we never visited them. They always came to us.

Windsor, it is often said, is a place that people pass through, and until I moved here, I was no different. My first visit through the city was in 2012 to attend a Tigers game. I was attending the University of Waterloo at the time, and wasn't really into sports, but my friend Peter, an American, was a huge Tigers fan. The ticket was cheap and I was curious to see what existed past London on the other side of the 401, so I agreed to tag along. What I saw of Windsor was fleeting, consisting of the minutes spent between the highway and the tunnel tollbooth. While we had a great time at Comerica Park, I didn't expect that I'd be back in the area for a while.

I should have known better. After all, my life has been full of unexpected turns. Working for the CBC, as just one example, was not part of my original life plan.

When I was taking in that Tigers game, I had a bachelor's degree from Canadian Studies from Trent University in Peterborough under my belt, and I was at the University of Waterloo to become an urban planner. I've always been an urbanist at heart, and my idea of a dream job was working as a planner for a public transit agency, helping people get around more efficiently. I had certainly never considered journalism as a career.

The only reason I found myself anywhere close to the CBC was because of a program called the Gzowski Internship. It's a paid, four-month position offered to one graduate each from a group of four universities, including Trent. The idea is to bring a non-journalist into CBC Radio, give them a crash course in radio production, and throw them right into the newsroom. Having grown up on CBC radio and television, I'd always wanted to see what happened behind the scenes of my favourite shows, so I applied, thinking it would be a fun summer work experience before I headed off to grad school. It ended up changing my life.

The people at CBC Toronto's radio shows took a liking to me, and even after I moved a few hours away to Waterloo, would call on me regularly to fill in for people who were sick or on vacation. Having developed a love for the art of radio, I readily agreed, dropping whatever I was doing in Waterloo and hopping onto a bus—even if it was for only a day of work. Eventually, I realized that while I loved urban planning, I loved exploring urban issues—and other ideas—with a radio audience more. I began to look for jobs with the CBC, and happened to see one in Windsor. Robin Brown, who had hosted *Here & Now*, CBC Radio's afternoon show in Toronto, while I was an intern, had recently moved to Windsor to become the producer of the morning show, at the time known as *The Early Shift*. Realizing that I knew at least one familiar face there, I decided to apply.

To my surprise, I was selected for an interview. While I could have done it over the phone, I decided to make the drive down the 401 and do it in person. I hoped that by doing so I'd show CBC's local brass my commitment—and I wanted to see what Windsor was like, anyway.

In the weeks prior to my interview, I did a lot of research on Windsor, trying to get a handle on what it would be like to live there. Most of what I read online was not flattering: chronic unemployment, empty streets. What I read of its American neighbour didn't help, either.

I began to worry. I arrived in Windsor a few hours ahead of the interview, hoping to size the city up firsthand. It was a gorgeous, still-summery September. It was a heck of a lot warmer than it was three hours up the road in Waterloo. I drove, walked, and wandered, more and more surprised by what I saw, revising my thoughts and expectations of the city on the spot.

Yes, there were vacant storefronts. Yes, the roads were a little bumpy. But this wasn't the dark, depressing place I'd expected. There were people on the sidewalks, shops were bustling, transit buses were picking up passengers. There was a diversity of people, food, and languages. As I explored downtown, I marvelled at the partially pedestrianized Maiden Lane, admiring the historic Lazare's Furs sign, the street art,

the mere existence of such an alley. One of my favourite types of urban spaces, alleys were few and far between in Peterborough and in many of the other cities in which I've either lived or visited. Here, it seemed, they were everywhere. The urbanist in me was thrilled.

I popped into the Squirrel Cage—then a relatively new operation—for lunch, and was impressed with the hope that owners and recent Toronto transplants John Ansell and Steven Thompson had for Windsor. Heading to the CBC on Riverside Drive, I was even more surprised with the riverfront. Flowers were blooming. People were jogging and cycling. Others were eating lunch and taking in the breathtaking view of the Detroit skyline.

This was definitely not the Windsor that had come through in my research. When I was offered the job, I said yes without hesitation.

So when people reacted negatively to the news of my upcoming move, I told them about the city I saw on my first "real" visit. Sure, it was only a first impression, but it was a good one. Like the owners of the Squirrel Cage, I saw a lot of potential.

Food has been central to my life for as long as I can remember.

My dad is a chef, and my mom an equally incredible cook. Both immigrated to Canada from India in the early 1980s, armed with university degrees that weren't recognized here. Like countless other immigrants to Canada, they were forced to make the best of it.

My mom became an administrative assistant, first at the local health unit, and then at the university. My dad got into the food industry, first in a bakery, then a pizzeria, and for the majority of his career at a popular steakhouse.

He ended up going to college in Peterborough to get his formal culinary qualifications.

At home, the food we ate was inspired by the world. Indian food was predominant, though we were just as likely to feast on a rich *spaghetti bolognese* as we were rice and *pork baffat*. Fusion, though we may not have called it that at the time, was key. Traditions merged and blended, fused, becoming something uniquely their own, as often as flavours did. At Thanksgiving, for example, the turkey remained the star of the feast in a nod to my parents' adopted home, but it was marinated in a spicy masala for days, allowing the meat, stuffing, and gravy a uniquely Indian flavour. The kitchen, not the living or family room, was the central meeting place of my childhood home, the place where anything could happen, and quite often did. My sense of culinary adventure—that willingness to try anything at least once—is a direct result of my parents' willingness to try new food themselves.

Despite having fantastic food at home, I still loved going to restaurants—and for a city a fraction of the size of Windsor, let alone Toronto, Peterborough was a great place to eat. As a second-year student, I had the opportunity to review restaurants for *Arthur,* Trent University's student newspaper. Despite the fact that Peterborough had two newspapers owned by major media companies, I was the only restaurant critic in the city. I kept the gig until the day I graduated. When I arrived in Windsor, *The Early Shift* was in the middle of a program renewal. Even the name was up for debate—it ended up being changed to *Windsor Morning* less than a year after I arrived.

Hoping to develop more Windsor-based radio columnists, producer Robin Brown and managing editor Shawna Kelly noticed the restaurant-critic gig on my resumé and asked if I'd be willing to develop a regular local food column. It wouldn't be something as formal as restaurant reviews; rather, the segment was to focus on the food culture of the region. The idea, as it was pitched to me at the time, was to offer a series of informal portraits in which I would explore my new home through its food. I readily agreed: I'd been touring some of the local restaurants and cafés anyway. I figured I could manage a few dozen stories before the feature petered out. A few years and well over one hundred stories later, I now realize that I've only just scratched the surface.

I often get asked what my favourite aspect of Windsor's food scene is. Without a doubt, it's the people. This region is filled with tales that you just can't find anywhere else. Where else can a policy analyst become a bagel maker? A bartender turn into a charcuterie maker? A tool and die shop expand into flour production? Windsor and Essex County is filled with improbable, incredible food stories—and we're all the richer for it.

This cookbook is a reflection of my continuing discovery of the food and people that make Windsor-Essex great. By no means is it exhaustive; there are still many restaurants I have yet to try, farmers I have yet to meet, and only so many stories that can fit in this book. Also, some places simply weren't willing to share their recipes. But those who have offer all the proof we need of the richness of Windsor's food culture.

I envision this cookbook as a bit of a culinary tour guide, a testament to the passion and the possibility I encounter on a daily basis. People who work for hours, weeks, and years to make a product that they can be proud of and that you can enjoy. I hope some of that passion and possibility rubs off on you. It certainly has on me.

Anchor Coffee House

2187 Huron Church Road, Unit 230
(519) 966-0888
anchorcoffeehouse.com

I THINK IT'S SAFE to say that for most of us Huron Church Road conjures up images of motels, fast food joints and of course, the Ambassador Bridge. It was certainly my impression of the place when I moved here back in 2012.

Not much has changed today—except one thing. Huron Church Road is also where you'll find Windsor's best third-wave coffee house, nestled improbably between an Applebees and a generic suite of offices that once housed a number of Herb Gray Parkway staff.

Anchor Coffee House is the bricks and mortar result of a journey that started for Kyle and Rachel Bondy in high school, where, as friends, the idea of owning a coffee shop began. At the risk of sounding clichéd, friendship turned into dating, dating turned into marriage and the young couple started working on making their dream of owning a coffee shop a reality.

Like many of the recent crop of successful Windsor food businesses, Anchor Coffee House started in 2013 as a booth at the Downtown Windsor Farmers' Market; Kyle describes it as a way of testing the market.

Saying it went well seems a bit of an understatement—by January 2014, just a few months later, Anchor Coffee House opened as a full-blown operation on Huron Church. It replaced a struggling café that Rachel worked at as an employee.

I first walked into Anchor Coffee House a few weeks after it opened, when they invited a local roaster to hold a coffee tasting seminar. Considering the place had just opened, I was

What thrills me most about Anchor is how they manage to balance consistency with a healthy sense of discovery. A multi-roaster café, the Anchor team is constantly bringing in new beans from Canada's best roasters. While this means that the coffee is always changing, the selection is curated to the point where you never need to be concerned about encountering a bad brew.

shocked by the number in attendance—it was packed.

Despite its small size and unusual location, Anchor Coffee House has managed to build a sense of place in a part of the city that sorely lacks it. That sense of community has turned into a loyal and growing clientele; in fact, Ryan Larocque, a recent University of Windsor business grad and now co-owner of the business, started off as regular customer.

Unlike so many third-wave coffee houses, the non-beverage side of the operation isn't an afterthought. Just about everything at Anchor is made from scratch; if it's not made in-house, it comes from incredible local suppliers like The Earnest Bagel Co. (see pages 80-85) and Blak's Bakery (see pages 28-33). Avid travellers, Kyle and Rachel are constantly trying the latest and greatest not just in Windsor and Detroit, but across North America, often bringing the best of what they taste-test back to the Anchor menu.

Anchor Spiced Granola

YIELD: 9 CUPS

4 cups rolled oats
1 1/2 cups walnuts
1 1/2 cups pecans
1 1/2 cups whole almonds
2 tsp ground cinnamon
1 tsp ground nutmeg
1 tsp sea salt
1/3 cup boiled water
1 1/2 cups brown sugar
1/3 cup olive oil
2 tsp vanilla extract

Pre-heat oven to 250 degrees.

Mix together oats, walnuts, pecans, almonds, cinnamon, nutmeg, and salt in a large bowl.

Whisk boiling water and brown sugar until sugar is dissolved. Add oil and vanilla, mixing well, creating a syrupy mixture.

Pour syrup over oats and nuts. Mix well until evenly coated.

Line baking sheet with parchment paper and spread granola evenly.

Bake one hour. Remove from oven and flip. Bake another 45 minutes to one hour.

Espresso Shortbread Squares

YIELD: 9 SQUARES

2 cups butter, softened
2 cups brown sugar
4 fl oz espresso
2 tsp vanilla extract
4 cups flour
1 tsp baking powder
1 tsp sea salt
1 cup semi-sweet chocolate chips

Pre-heat oven to 375 degrees.

Cream together butter and sugar.

Add espresso and vanilla extract.

Mix in flour, baking powder, and sea salt.

Stir in chocolate chips until mixed evenly throughout dough.

Press dough in a 11 x 13 baking pan lined with parchment paper.

Bake 20 minutes. Cool completely before cutting.

Cold Brew Coffee

1/4 cup of coarsely ground coffee (your preference)
1 litre of filtered water

Take whole bean coffee of choice (preferably within 2 weeks of roast date), grind coarse (equivalent of french-press ground), and put in container (1 litre mason jar works well). Pour cold-filtered water over coffee grounds. Agitate coffee with mixing spoon to ensure coffee grounds are evenly covered. Put lid on container and let sit at room temperature for 12-24 hours, depending on preferred strength. When satisfied with extraction taste, pour jar contents through coffee filter or cheesecloth to strain out sediment and grounds. Keep refrigerated.

Unlike traditional iced coffee, cold brewed coffee is wonderfully mellow. A great beverage for a hot Windsor-Essex summer.

Arcata Pizzeria / Volcano Pizza

3021 Dougall Avenue, Windsor
(519) 969-2551
arcatapizzeria.com

ASK TEN WINDSORITES for their favourite pizza place, and you'll get ten different answers. It's not surprising—the quality of pizza in this city is very high. As long as you stay away from the national chains, you're almost guaranteed to get a great pizza.

A lot of people ask me what makes Windsor-style pizza different from those of other regions, either in Canada or elsewhere. It's a bit of a contentious question, but here are my thoughts on the matter.

- Use of a deck oven. Many pizza places in Canada use the inferior conveyor ovens, which are simpler to use. Deck ovens require more care—but the end result is much better.
- Medium-crust pizza. Windsor-style pizza isn't exactly thin-crust, but it doesn't have massive dough crust ends either.
- Shredded pepperoni, often referred to on the menu as "sausage". Circular pepperoni is not permitted.
- Canned mushrooms. I thought this was pretty unappetizing at first, but I understand the logic now—they don't shrivel up like fresh mushrooms under heat.
- Local cheese. If the pizza doesn't use locally-produced mozzarella from the Galati Cheese Company, it's not Windsor-style pizza. Galati Cheese makes two brands of mozzarella—Galati and Uniondale. I prefer the higher-fat Uniondale.

Arcata Pizzeria is one of the older pizzerias in the city, opening its doors in late 1950s—and as far as my criteria is concerned, it checks all the boxes.

Walking in on a busy Friday or Saturday night is a little surreal. The small kitchen is jam-packed with up to a dozen staff, busy with the various stages of pizza production.

Most jarring of all is the silence.

It's not that the staff is having a miserable time—they're just deep in the pizza-making zone. The atmosphere is serene, almost church-like. You can feel their reverence for the almighty pie.

Arcata is a well-oiled, pizza-making machine—and its high priest, if you will, is Bob Abumeeiz.

Bob has owned Arcata Pizza for about twenty years, and he's been in the kitchen for just about every one of those days. A self-proclaimed perfectionist, Bob, who came to Windsor from Libya in the 1980s, is deeply passionate about the pizzas he produces. And it shows. He regularly gets calls from customers from as far afield as Alberta while visiting family in Windsor to prepare pre-baked pizzas that they can take home. His pizza even made national news when a Windsor ex-pat living in Regina spent $140—including $84 in shipping—to ship a party-sized pizza for the Super Bowl.

Ask Bob what the secret to his pizza is and he points to the sauce. 50% of a pizza's taste is sauce, he claims; and his thick, spicy sauce is where he stakes his reputation. I also think the dough makes his pizzas great; it's much tastier than that of many other pizzerias in town. Part of the reason for this is that it proofs—or rests—for 3 days before it makes it into an oven.

While Bob was gracious enough to share some of the most interesting entries on his menu, he wasn't willing to share his recipe for the actual pizza. It's understandable—in a city with more pizza shops than you can shake a stick at, the small elements that make your pie different is what drives repeat sales.

Arcata wasn't the originator of the Windsor-style pie. When I asked Bob to trace the lineage of his pie, he pointed to Volcano Pizza.

Located at the corner of Wyandotte and Victoria, Volcano Pizzeria, like Arcata, opened in the late 1950s. Named after Mount Vesuvius, Volcano was owned by Italian immigrants Frank Gualteri and Gino Manzo. While not the first pizzeria in the city, it's an establishment Windsorites of a certain generation associate with the dish. Part of this is certainly due to Volcano's iconic delivery service, which was made up of fleet of Jeeps and Volkswagen Beetles.

According to Ada, Frank's widow, Frank learned how to make pizza from a cousin who owned a pizzeria in Detroit. While I can't definitively say this is where Windsor-style pizza comes from, the family tells me that their pizza had all the hallmarks of what makes this style unique: canned mushrooms (fresh mushrooms get too dry), shredded pepperoni (easier and faster to spread evenly) and local mozzarella on a crispy medium crust, all baked in a deck oven.

The Gualteri family was only too happy to share the recipe for this book—they say that many of Frank's employees went out to start pizzerias of their own. In fact, Frank's daughter Adele, who grew up working as a server at Volcano, taught the family recipe as a family studies teacher in LaSalle.

Spaghetti Sauce

1 oz vegetable oil
1 onion (finely chopped)
2-4 cloves garlic (minced)
1/2 tsp crushed peppers
1/2 lb ground beef
1/2 lb ground veal
16 oz tomato purée
6 oz tomato paste
16 oz roasted tomato purée
1/4 cup water
1 sprig rosemary
2 tsp sugar (or to taste)
1 tsp salt (or to taste)

Heat oil in large sauce pan over medium heat. Add onion, garlic, and crushed pepper. Stir and cook until onions are translucent, approximately 10 minutes.

Add ground beef and ground veal. Cook and stir until meat browns. Drain grease.

Add tomato purée, tomato paste, roasted tomato purée, and water. Lower heat and simmer uncovered for a half hour, stirring occasionally.

Add sprig of rosemary. Simmer additional half hour.

Remove sauce from heat. Let cool. Add sugar and salt to taste.

Serve with favourite your pasta.

Garlic Sauce

4 fresh peeled garlic cloves
2 egg whites
1/2 lemon (juiced)
2 cups mazola oil

Blend cloves of garlic in a blender for 5 minutes or until they are well-blended. Add 2 egg whites and blend for additional minute. While blending, add lemon juice and slowly pour in mazola oil. Let it fold into the mixture for 2–3 minutes. Once finished, refrigerate until ready to use.

* In the summer it is recommended to add some ice cubes to avoid any separation in the mixture.

Volcano Pizza (from Adele Gualtieri-Amato)

YIELD: 1 PIZZA

Dough:
2 3/4 - 3 1/4 cups all-purpose flour
1 package active dry yeast
1/4 tsp salt
1 cup warm water
2 tbsp olive oil
cornmeal (optional)

Sauce:
1 can crushed tomatoes (28 oz)
1 tbsp olive oil
1 1/2 tsp garlic powder
2 tsp dried oregano
1/2 tsp salt (to taste)

Combine 1¼ cups of flour, yeast, and salt in a large mixing bowl. Add water and oil. With an electric mixer beat on low for 30 seconds, scraping bowl. Beat on high for 3 minutes. With wooden spoon, stir in as much of the remaining flour as you can.

Turn dough out on a lightly floured surface. Knead, adding flour as needed, to make a moderately stiff dough that is smooth and elastic (6–8 minutes total). Cover and let rest 10 minutes.

Grease a medium pizza pan. If desired, sprinkle with cornmeal. Roll dough into a circle. Transfer to prepared pan. Build up edges slightly. Do not let rise.

Add sauce, cheese and toppings. Uniondale-brand mozzarella (produced in Windsor by Galati Cheese) and Success-brand canned mushrooms are recommended. Bake at 450 degrees for 15 minutes or until bubbly.

BiBim To Go

2175 Wyandotte Street West, Windsor
(519) 915-1797
facebook.com/Bibim-To-
Go-133868716706844/

WHEN I MOVED to Windsor to work for the CBC, the apartment for which I signed a lease wasn't going to be ready for the better part of a month. Thankfully, my building had a guest suite my wife Leslie and I could use in the interim. It was small but inexpensive, and had a lovely, 16th-floor view of Windsor.

There was just one problem: no kitchen. Not even a hot plate. I could assemble basic breakfasts and lunch thanks to a little bar fridge, but the lack of a proper space to prepare anything more than a sandwich meant we had to go out for dinner every single night.

While it certainly wasn't easy on the pocketbook, this extended period of restaurant dining provided a crash course in Windsor's food scene. One of the first restaurants that really demonstrated the depth of this city's culinary chops was BiBim To Go.

Located in the heart of the Wyandotte Street commercial district, close to the University, BiBim To Go specializes in bibimbap, a classic Korean dish made of warm rice, some sort of protein, various julienned vegetables, and gochujang, a fermented chili paste. Most commonly, this dish is made with marinated beef and topped with a fried egg, served sunny side up. In restaurants, bibimbap is often served in a piping hot stone bowl, which has the added benefit of making the rice crispy and even hotter.

If I had to pick a single national cuisine to eat for the rest of my life, it may very well be Korean. With its heavy use of chilis, meat, rice and fermented condiments like kimchi, Korean food contains just about everything I love about food. Bibimbap combines many of these aspects in one meal, making this my all-time favourite Korean dish. It's even pretty healthy.

So when I discovered that Windsor had a restaurant that specialized in variations of my favourite meal, I was thrilled. I'd never seen anything like it before. In addition to the traditional beef, BiBim To Go offered mushroom, tofu and pork variations, to name just a few.

Originally from Korea, owner Julianna Noh came to Canada in 2002 with her twin daughters, Maria and Martha, who are visually impaired. Julianna and her family ended up in Windsor when her daughters were accepted at the University of Windsor to study music.

With all of six tables, eating at BiBim To Go is a little like eating at the cozy house of your Korean aunt. Just about everything is made from scratch, including Juliana's fantastic kimchi, a spicy fermented cabbage, which I adore. It's served with every lovingly prepared, artfully arranged meal, along with a number of other tiny dishes known as banchan.

The fact that Windsor could support a restaurant like BiBim To Go gave me a lot of hope about the state of the food scene in my new home. It became the subject of my first radio column, and has occupied a place in my heart ever since.

Bibimbap

YIELD: 5 SERVINGS

Marinade:

1 tbsp soy sauce

1 tbsp sugar

1/4 can pineapples (minced)

1 tsp minced garlic

sesame oil

black pepper

6 oz beef sirloin (substitute tofu or mushroom)

5 dried shitake mushrooms

2 cucumbers

salt (to taste)

4 cups short grain rice

4 3/4 cups water

7 oz soybean sprouts

sesame oil

2 1/2 tsp garlic (minced)

7 oz mung bean sprouts

2 medium zucchinis

pepper (to taste)

soy sauce (to taste)

2 medium carrots

Sauce:

5 tbsp Gochujang (Korean red chili pepper paste)

1 tbsp maltose syrup

1 tbsp water

5 eggs

sesame seeds

Marinade:

Combine soy sauce, sugar, pineapples, garlic, sesame oil, and black pepper.

Sauce:

Mix gochujang, maltose syrup, and water. Set aside

Cut beef into 2-inch thin long strips and then mix in marinade. Let sit for 2–3 hours.

Soak shitake mushrooms in warm water for 2–3 hours.

Cut cucumbers in half lengthwise and thinly slice. Sprinkle salt over sliced cucumbers and then set aside for 2–3 hours.

Cook the rice in a rice cooker with 4¾ cups of water for a drier rice.

Boil soybean sprouts for 2–3 minutes. Drain. Soak in cold water for 2 minutes. Drain. Season with 1 tsp sesame oil, 1 tsp minced garlic, and salt to taste.

Boil mung bean sprouts for 2–3 minutes. Drain. Soak in cold water for 2 minutes. Drain. Season with 1 tsp sesame oil, 1 tsp minced garlic, and salt to taste.

Squeeze cucumbers and season with ½ tsp minced garlic, 1 tsp sesame oil, and a pinch of salt.

Halve and slice zucchini. Add ½ tsp minced garlic, 1 tsp sesame oil, a pinch of pepper. Sauté in a lightly oiled skillet 1–2 minutes over medium-high heat.

Sauté beef over high heat, aproximately 2 minutes.

Squeeze shitake mushrooms and cut thinly. Sauté in a lightly oiled skillet for 3–4 minutes with a little sesame oil, soy sauce, and minced garlic.

In an oiled skillet over medium heat, sauté carrots until softened. Season with salt, black pepper, sesame oil, and minced garlic.

Heat stone bowl over medium heat until very hot. Place cooked rice at the bottom and wait a few minutes until the rice sizzles. Neatly arrange a small amount of each prepared vegetable and the beef. Drizzle with sauce and top with a fried egg sunny side up. Garnish with sesame oil and roasted sesame seeds.

Easy Kimchi

YIELD: 1 JAR

1 medium napa cabbage

1/2 cup salt

12 cups water

1/2 medium daikon radish (peeled and julienned)

1/2 cup Korean red pepper powder

1 tbsp fermented baby shrimp

4-5 green onions (sliced)

1 tsp sugar

1 tbsp garlic (minced)

Quarter cabbage lengthwise and remove cores. Slice into 2–3 cm wide strips. Mix in large bowl with salt and cover with water. Let sit at room temperature for 2–3 hours.

Mix radish with Korean red pepper powder, fermented baby shrimp, and a pinch of salt. Let sit at room temperature for 2–3 hours.

Thoroughly rinse the cabbage in cold water 3–4 times and drain. Combine with radish mixture until cabbage is thoroughly coated. Mix in green onion, sugar, and garlic.

Seal in a glass jar and store at room temperature for 7 days to ferment. Refrigerate for up to 1 month. Kimchi is best after approximately two weeks (most lactobacillus).

Soft Tofu Soup

YIELD: 4 SERVINGS

4 tsp vegetable oil

8 tbsp thinly sliced kimchi (recipe page 26)

4 oz thinly sliced pork

4 tsp minced garlic

4 tsp fish sauce

2 tbsp red chili pepper powder

4 cups of water

4 12 oz packages soft tofu

4 sliced white mushrooms (optional)

2 green onions

4 eggs

Drizzle vegetable oil in a large pot over medium heat. Stir in kimchi, pork, garlic, fish sauce, and chili powder. Cook, stirring occasionally, until pork is browned, approximately 3–5 minutes.

Add water and boil for 3–4 minutes. Add soft tofu and mushroom, then boil for additional 4–5 minutes.

Add green onion and egg, immediately remove from heat. Let sit for 2 minutes and serve, ensuring one poached egg is placed in each bowl.

*A great source for local tofu is Ruey-Feng Trading Company on Tecumseh Road in Windsor.

Blak's Bakery

1022 Langlois Avenue, Windsor
(519) 253-4344
blaksbakery.com

WINDSOR IS FULL of great bakeries. I could probably write an entire book about them. Alas, for this project, I had to cut it down to the essentials.

Founded in 1918, Blak's Bakery is one of the oldest bakeries in the region and quite possibly one of the oldest in the country. The place is a local institution. Any book about Windsor would be remiss to exclude it. They're probably best known for pączkis, those filled Polish doughnuts that this region goes crazy for every Shrove Tuesday. It's a tradition I enjoy, because I'm not a huge fan of pancakes.

But during the rest of the year, Blak's really means bread.

Especially rye bread. Blak's offer about a dozen varieties of rye bread, baked in the same oven used on the day they opened. According to owner Tony Blak—whose grandfather Peter started the bakery after immigrating from Poland via Rochester, NY and Detroit—their heritage Petersen oven is likely one of the last left in North America. Originally coke fired, the oven was converted to coal and then, in the 1960s, to natural gas.

But the sense of history doesn't end with where the bread is baked. Blak's sour—or bread starter—is a living culture that comprises an essential part each loaf. It's been growing continuously since 1918, regenerating and absorbing the natural yeasts found in the area of Langlois and Erie Street. It's not a stretch to say that if the bakery were to move to a different part of the city, the bread may very well taste a little different.

Every day, Blak's Bakery produces hundreds of bread loaves, as well as various cookies and other pastries. Many are sold at the bakery, others are sold at local grocery stores, and you'll find their products at a fair number of Windsor restaurants and delis. Nothing makes me happier than to walk into a sandwich shop and see a nice big loaf of marble or caraway seed rye from Blak's on the counter. Like the gluten in their breads, Blak's Bakery binds this city together.

And it's not just Windsorites who love the bread—Jessica Seinfeld, wife of comedian Jerry Seinfeld, heaped praised on Blak's marble rye recently after her famous husband brought some home after a show in Windsor.

"Every once in awhile, Jerry comes home from being on the road with something really good," she wrote. "This time, it was the most gorgeous and delicious marble rye bread from Blak's Bakery in Windsor, Ontario. If I lived there, I'd be smearing butter on this bread all day long."

I couldn't agree more.

Polish Egg-Twist Bread (Chałka)

YIELD: 1 LOAF

Dough:
1 cup water
1 1/2 tbsp sugar
1 tbsp dry yeast
1 egg
1 1/4 tsp salt
1 1/2 tbsp canola oil
1 3/4 cups bread flour

Egg Wash Topping:
1 egg plus 1 yolk
1 tsp water
sesame seeds (for sprinkling)

In a large bowl mix together water, sugar, and yeast. Let stand for 10 minutes. Whisk in one whole egg.

Add salt and canola oil. Fold in flour. Knead for 8–12 minutes, until dough is supple and can be stretched to look translucent.

Put dough in large greased bowl. Lightly spray dough with canola oil, cover with plastic wrap, and place in a warm part of the kitchen away from any drafts. Let rise for about an hour until it doubles in size.

Knock down dough and place on lightly floured surface. Divide into three pieces. Roll them into strips about 6 inches long, cover with plastic on counter and let stand 15 minutes.

Roll them out to about 14 inches, and braid them. Place the dough on a parchment-lined pan.

Whisk 1 egg, 1 yolk, and water. Brush over braided loaf. Cover with plastic wrap, and place in a warm part of the kitchen away from drafts. Let rise for about an hour until it doubles in size.

Pre-heat oven to 350 degrees.

Brush egg-wash over braided loaf for a second time. Place pan in middle of oven. Bake for 30 minutes, to an internal temperature of 200 degrees.

Let cool completely before slicing. Can be used the next day for amazing French toast.

Blak's Best Date Squares

YIELD: 16 SQUARES

Filling:
1 cup dates
1 cup water
2 1/2 tbps brown sugar
1 tbsp lemon juice

Pastry Crumb:
1/2 cup pastry flour
1/2 cup whole wheat flour
1/2 tsp salt
1 cup butter
1/2 cup rolled oats
1 cup brown sugar
3 tbsp shredded fine coconut

Filling:
Place dates in medium pot and cover with water. Bring to a boil. Reduce heat and simmer, stirring often, until dates are easily smashed. Stir in brown sugar and lemon juice. Set aside to cool. Press mixture through medium-holed strainer to capture any pits. May be made a day in advance, and left in fridge to cool.

Pastry Crumb:
In large bowl whisk pastry flour, whole wheat flour, and salt.

Cut butter into dry mixture until lumps are the size of peas.

Gently fold in oats, brown sugar, and coconut. Do not over-mix, must look like crumbs.

Divide crumbs in half. Distribute ½ of the crumbs on the bottom of a buttered 8 x 8 baking pan. Press crumbs down, making a flat even surface on the bottom of the pan.

Carefully spread date mixture over the crumbs, making sure not to drag the crumbs off the bottom. Even the date mixture with a spatula.

Spread remaining crumbs over the date mixture. Lightly pat crumbs down so as not to have filling squeeze through.

Pre-heat oven to 350 degrees. Bake for 25 to 30 minutes, until crumbs turn very light brown.

Let pan completely cool before cutting into squares.

Country Rye

YIELD: 2 LOAVES

2 1/2 tsp yeast
1/2 cup rye sour bram
2 1/2 cups dark rye flour
2 3/4 cups water
2 1/2 tsp oz salt
2 1/2 cups plus 4 tbsp bread flour

*With a days notice rye sour bram can be purchased from Blak's Bakery

Combine yeast, rye sour bram, 1½ cup of dark rye flour, and 1¼ cups water. Let sit for approximately 4 hours.

In upright mixer add 1 cup dark rye flour, bread flour, 1½ cups water, and salt to yeast mixture. Mix with dough hook on low until well incorporated (approximately 8 minutes). Let rest 15 minutes.

Divide dough in half and round into boules. Place on baking sheet sprinkled with corn meal, spray with oil, cover with plastic wrap, and let rest in warm part of kitchen for 45 minutes.

Pre-heat oven to 425 degrees and place a baking sheet of water on the bottom rack. Cut 4 lines from centre in dough. Bake on middle rack for approximately 25 minutes, until the internal temperature reaches 200 degrees.

The Blind Owl

430 Ouellette Ave, Windsor
facebook.com/blindowlbar

I'M NOT A huge drinker—but when I do imbibe, I gravitate toward cocktails. Windsor, as I'm fond of telling people, is a city built on drinking (distilling) and driving (minivans)—but until recently, I did most of my cocktail consumption in Detroit. There simply weren't many places to get a good, expertly prepared craft cocktail on this side of the river.

Enter The Blind Owl.

Mark Dutka is the brains behind The Blind Owl, a family business he operates with Lucas, his brother-in-law. It's not a stretch to say that bartending is in Mark's DNA—he's a third-generation bartender. His family owned Abars for years—that's the (in)famous riverfront watering hole where Al Capone reportedly did business during Prohibition. After it was sold, Mark tended bar for a number of local restaurants, including Rino's Kitchen (see pages 154-159) and The Willistead (see pages 166-171).

I first met Mark when I was doing a story about Hung Meats, a small business he used to run that was dedicated to his other passion: artisanal, small-batch charcuterie. When I heard Mark was opening a place downtown serving craft cocktails AND his fantastic cured meats, I was over the moon. This was exactly what Windsor needed.

Like any proper speakeasy, The Blind Owl is a little hard to find. Located in the same building as the Holiday Inn on Ouellette Ave, it's easy to walk right past and ignore the yellow stucco exterior. You'd think that would be a business-killer, but somehow, it works—just about every time I've visited, the dark, intimate 30-seat space is packed.

The Blind Owl specializes in cocktails with roots before or during prohibition. With the exception of the alcohol itself, just about everything—the syrups, the bitters, even the vinegars used in the shrubs—are made in-house. As Mark puts it, this is a cocktail lounge with restaurant-style service. I love Mark's take on cocktail classics. The Smokey Sour Cocktail is a fantastic example of how to spice up your run-of-the-mill bourbon sour. Like many restaurants, the offerings change seasonally—a cocktail you order in the dog days of summer may not be available in the middle of January. It also means that your drink may take a little longer to get to your table than it would at your neighbourhood pub.

But trust me—the wait is worth it.

Hung Meats Real Deal Bacon

YIELD: 5 POUNDS

5 lbs of pork belly
1/4 cup kosher salt
1/2 cup sugar or maple syrup
1/4 tsp pink salt

In extra large ziplock bag mix kosher salt, sugar (or syrup) and pink salt. Add pork belly to mixture and massage until completely coated.

Store in fridge for 10 days. The cure will draw out a fair amount of liquid: this is normal and the liquid should be left in the bag until the curing process is finished. Flip the bag in the fridge every second day.

Remove from the bag and rinse thoroughly with cold water to wash off the cure.

Let the cured pork belly dry on a rack for approximately 1–2 hours, until a little sticky to the touch.

Smoke in smoker or bbq at 200–225 degrees over indirect heat for 3–4 hours or until the internal temperature is 150. (Apple-wood chips are preferrable). Cool and slice.

The bacon will keep for 1–2 weeks in the fridge or can be frozen for up to 3 months.

Other flavours may be added to the cure such as black pepper, thyme, coriander etc.

Smokey Sour Cocktail

YIELD: 1 SERVING

Cinnamon syrup:
1/2 cup sugar
1/2 cup water
3 cinnamon sticks

Black Tea Syrup:
1/2 cup sugar
1/2 cup water
4 black tea bags

Cocktail:
2 oz bourbon
3/4 oz fresh lemon juice
1/2 oz cinnamon syrup
1/4 oz black tea syrup
1/2 oz egg white
smoking cinnamon stick garnish

Cinnamon Syrup:
Over medium-high heat bring sugar, water, and cinnamon sticks to boil. Reduce heat to low and simmer, stirring constantly, until sugar is completely dissolved and mixture is clear, approximately 3–5 minutes.

Black Tea Syrup:
Over medium-high heat bring sugar, water, and tea to boil. Reduce heat to low and simmer, stirring constantly, until sugar is completely dissolved and mixture is clear, approximately 3–5 minutes.

Cocktail:
Shake all ingredients minus the cinnamon stick in an ice-filled cocktail shaker. Strain into glass and dump ice out of shaker, pour ingredients back into empty shaker and shake hard once more. This is called a dry shake and adds body and froth to the finished product.

Pour into an ice-filled rocks glass and garnish with cinnamon stick. Light end of cinnamon stick aflame.

Spa Water Cocktail

YIELD: 1 SERVING

Simple Syrup:
1/2 cup sugar
1/2 cup water

Cocktail:
2 oz vodka
1/2 oz fresh lemon juice
1/2 oz simple syrup
1/4 tsp matcha green tea powder
2 cucumber slices
1 bunch mint

Syrup:

Over medium-high heat bring sugar and water to boil. Reduce heat to low and simmer, stirring constantly, until sugar is completely dissolved and mixture is clear, approximately 3–5 minutes.

Cocktail:

Muddle cucumber and mint in the bottom of a cocktail shaker, add ice and the rest of the ingredients. Shake hard. Strain into ice-filled Collins glass and add a slice of cucumber and mint leaf for garnish.

Caribbean Island Spice

1725 Wyandotte Street West, Windsor
(519) 915-5837
instagram.com/caribbeanislandspice

MANY RESTAURANTS TRY really hard to create a dining or serving area that transports you away. Sometimes it works—but in my experience, it usually ends up looking a little kitschy.

These places could learn a lesson in effortless atmosphere from Caribbean Island Spice.

The bright, cheerful décor of the Wyandotte Street eatery didn't cost a lot. There are no tables or chairs, so you don't spend a lot of time there—it's purely takeout. But even a quick visit to the tiny restaurant evokes a feeling of being even further south than Windsor.

An island radio-station—complete with ads—blares over the stereo. Staff laugh and joke with customers, many of whom are clearly regulars. You can't help but grin.

The best part? The food is just as well-executed as the atmosphere.

I've been a fan of Jamaican food for a long time, ever since my mom—who eats even spicier than me—started experimenting with jerk pork chops at home. My entire family fell in love with the bold favours and the heat of those fantastic Scotch bonnet peppers.

In my experience, many Jamaican restaurants do one dish well, but the rest leave much to be desired. Maybe the jerk chicken is too dry. Or the meat patties aren't flaky enough.

This isn't an issue at Caribbean Island Spice. I still haven't tried everything on the menu, but I haven't had a single disappointment. The oxtail is incredible. Jerk chicken? Juicy and spicy. Even the rice and peas, a common side dish, is perfectly executed. This place just oozes flavour.

Barbara Patterson and Jason Collins are the mother-son team behind the restaurant. Jason is a serial entrepreneur, with businesses in Toronto, Windsor, and Michigan. Barbara has worked at a number of restaurants in Windsor—and is a hell of a cook. They opened the restaurant a few years ago as a way of sharing this gift with the city. Today, their clientele is a mix of students, people from the neighbourhood, and people who simply want a good lunch.

Just about everything is made from scratch—and it shows. You can't always get everything on the menu. In fact, when you walk in, don't even bother looking at the listing above the counter.

What you're looking for is a small black chalkboard with the word "Ready" which lists all the dishes available that day—not just specials. This is not a place to come with your heart set on a particular dish; you just have to go with the flow.

It was a bit of a struggle to get Jason and Barbara to agree to join this book; they hold onto their recipes tightly. After an extended period of begging, they agreed to take part.

You're welcome.

Curry Chicken

YIELD: 4 SERVINGS

3 lbs chicken

2 1/2 tbsp Betta pack Curry powder

2 medium onions

5 sprigs thyme

2 cloves garlic

1/4 tsp allspice

1 tsp black pepper

2 tsp Lawrys seasoning salt

2 cups water

2 white potatoes (chopped)

2 Jamaican Scotch bonnet peppers

Clean, skin, and cut chicken into 1-inch cubes and wash with vinegar. Drain, season with curry, onion, thyme, garlic, all-spice (optional), black pepper, and salt. Let marinate for at least 30 minutes.

Pour 3 tablespoons of oil in a skillet over medium-high heat. Add seasoned chicken. Lightly brown the chicken for 5–7 minutes.

Add water, potatoes, and Scotch bonnet peppers. Cook for 25 minutes.

Serve over white rice.

Ackee and Saltfish

1/2 lb saltfish

ackee fruit (fresh, or tinned)

1-2 tbsp extra virgin olive oil

1 medium onion (chopped)

2 cloves garlic

2 stalks scallion (chopped)

1 medium tomato (chopped)

1 tsp Scotch bonnet pepper
   (chopped finely)

salt and pepper to taste

Put saltfish to soak in cold water for about 1 hour. If using fresh ackee soak in cold water for an hour. Drain, put into a medium pot, cover with water, and boil until tender.

De-bone and flake the saltfish.

Heat oil and sauté onion, garlic, scallions, tomatoes, and Scotch bonnet peppers until tender, approximately 5–6 minutes.

Add flaked saltfish, ackee, and salt and pepper. Toss lightly, cover and simmer over low heat for approximately 2 minutes.

Serve with your choice of white rice, fried dumplings, boiled dumplings, or rice and peas.

Carrots N' Dates

2090 Wyandotte Street East, Windsor
(519) 962-5115
carrotsndates.com

IF I HAVEN'T made it clear by now, I'm not a vegetarian. Neither is anyone in my family. My job would be a lot harder if I was.

Despite this, I genuinely enjoy eating vegetarian food.

If my mom is reading this, she's probably rolling her eyes. She has every right. As a teenager, I complained bitterly if there wasn't meat in every meal. But as I grow older, I find myself craving a meal with just vegetables more often.

Growing up in an Indian household, vegetarian meals were generally as tasty and 'complete' as meat-based ones, so I never understood why some people who grew up on Western diets associated "vegetarian" with "flavourless".

Flavourless is certainly far from the case at Carrots N' Dates, a place I consider Windsor's premier vegan restaurant.

Whenever I have a vegetarian friend or colleague visit me in Windsor, Carrots N' Dates is the first place I take them. Like a number of places in this book, I first encountered Carrots N' Dates at the Downtown Windsor Farmers' Market, where owner Neviana Nedeltchev had a funky, wood-panelled trailer selling smoothies and other vegan treats.

Emboldened by the response at the market, Neviana opened a bricks and mortar location in Walkerville in late 2013. It's been a hit—so much so that just recently, she took over the larger space next door to keep up with demand.

Now, vegan is quite a bit more restrictive than simply vegetarian; it involves eschewing the use of any animal products or animal-derived materials. That means no cheese, cream or eggs. Carrots N' Dates is also gluten-free. Not being able to use wheat, eggs or milk is a complication that would frustrate many cooks.

Yet somehow, Neviana and her staff manage to churn out incredibly tasty, filling food, inspired by flavours from around the world. And it's not just smoothies and entrees—the desserts at Carrots N' Dates are quite incredible as well. I'm still a little unnerved at how delicious a vegan, gluten-free 'cheesecake' can be.

Atmosphere is an important part of any restaurant, and Carrots N' Dates also delivers on this front. This isn't your traditional Wyandotte Street storefront; nor is it a building surrounded by a sea of parking. Carrots N' Dates is located in the basement of the Blackburn Radio building at Argyle and Wyandotte, almost hidden from street level.

Despite its subterranean setting, the restaurant manages to be bright and cheerful. Underground retail is a rarity in Windsor, even in our oldest areas; it's lovely to see one of Windsor's best restaurants as an example of what these spaces have the potential to be.

Detox Green Juice

2 apples

2 large cucumbers

1 zucchini

1/4 lemon (peeled)

1/2 cup of cabbage

Core apples and remove any seeds.

Process apples, cucumber, zucchini, lemon, and cabbage through juicer.

Green Smoothie

1 cup water or 1 cup cooled green tea
1 handful of spinach
1 banana
1 cup frozen berries
1-2 kale leaves
1 lemon wedge

Put spinach, banana, berries, and kale in blender and pulse. Add water/green tea and juice from lemon wedge and blend to desired consistency.

Chia and Oat Pizza Crust

YIELD: 1 PIZZA

1/2 cup chia seeds
1/2 cup plus 2 tbsp oat flour
2 tbsp ground flax seed
1 tsp dried oregano
1 tsp dried basil
1 tsp garlic powder
1 1/2 tsp sea salt
4 tbsp buckwheat groats (optional)
1 1/2 cups water

In a large bowl mix chia seeds, oat flour, flax seed, oregano, basil, garlic powder, salt, and buckwheat groats.

Add water and mix thouroughly. Let sit until mixture thickens, approximately 7–10 minutes.

Line a cookie sheet with parchment paper and spread mixture evenly across.

Bake in oven at 300 degrees for 20 minutes or until desired crispiness. Add your favourite pizza toppings and bake for an additional 10 minutes.

The Carvery

1301 Wyandotte Street East, Windsor
(519) 915-8999
facebook.com/carverywindsor

WHEN I MOVED to Windsor in the fall of 2012, I didn't know very many people. My then fiancee Leslie accompanied me, so we had each other. And, of course, I had a job—my primary reason for moving to the area in the first place. I couldn't imagine making the move to what was at the time Canada's unemployment capital without some sort of work lined up.

Mike Cowan and Kun Sun did just that. Like me, they also didn't know anybody in Windsor when they arrived a year later, in the fall of 2013. In addition to each other, they had their two young children.

But a job? Not in the picture. Not even close.

Just thinking about it makes me nervous.

Shortly before they packed up and moved to Windsor, Mike and Kun ran a taco shop near Vancouver's popular Kitsilano Beach. The business was successful, but with the cost of business and raising a family in one of Canada's most expensive metropolitan areas steadily increasing, the couple started looking for more modestly priced locales.

Windsor, with its rock-bottom property values, was top of the list. Sight unseen, they sold their restaurant, packed the kids into a car and drove across the country. Living out of a hotel for the first little while, Mike and Kun found a home—a steal, compared to Vancouver!—and, eventually, a former sushi restaurant at the corner of Wyandotte and Hall to start a business in. Forget finding work. Mike and Kun were making their own jobs.

After months of renovations and red tape, Mike and Kun opened The Carvery in May 2014. Specializing in gourmet sandwiches, I have to admit that I was concerned about the long-term prospects of the place. It was outside of trendy Walkerville and could be easily missed by the people who frequent that area. The food it served didn't exactly fit the primarily Middle Eastern demographic of the Wyandotte Town Centre neighbourhood it was located in.

But good food is a universal language—and The Carvery has prospered. It's a simple formula. With the exception of their bread, everything is made in-house. Sauces. Soups. Salad dressing.

Portions and prices are both reasonable. Most importantly, the meats are all roasted in-house.

But even if the formula is simple, it doesn't mean that such an endeavour is easy to execute.

Mike and Kun met in the kitchens of British Columbia—and their combined culinary experience shows. Consistency is flawless. The food is just as good today as the day it opened—if not better. Changes to the menu are thoughtful and considered.

In the two years since they've opened, I've never had a bad meal at The Carvery. In a place where just about everything is made from scratch, where so much can go wrong, that's no mean feat.

Hot Bacon Dressing

YIELD: 4 CUPS

3 lbs bacon (1-inch chop)
1 large onion (diced)
1 garlic bulb (minced)
2 tsp thyme
1 cup olive oil
1 tsp black pepper
2 cups red wine vinegar

Cook bacon in a large pot over medium-high heat, approximately 10 minutes. Add onion. Cook, stirring occasionally, until onions caramelize, approximately 7–10 minutes.

Add garlic, thyme, olive oil, pepper, and red wine vinegar. Reduce to low heat and simmer until ingredients are combined, approximately 20–30 minutes.

Blend thoroughly. Add to your favourite salad.

Porchetta

5 lbs pork butt roast
1 cup grainy Dijon mustard
5 lbs pork belly (skin on)
1 tbsp crushed garlic
2 tbsp chopped rosemary
2 tbsp chopped thyme
2 tbsp chopped parsley
1 tbsp vegetable oil
salt
black pepper

Butterfly the pork butt until about an inch thick. Rub ½ cup mustard over both sides and sprinkle with garlic, rosemary, thyme, and parsley.

Rub inside of pork belly with ½ cup of mustard and sprinkle with garlic, rosemary, thyme, and parsley.

Roll up the butt and place it on on the inside of the belly. Roll the belly over the butt and tie in place with 3–4 pieces of butcher's twine.

Rub skin with vegetable oil and generously season with salt and pepper. Refrigerate for up to 24 hours.

Pre-heat oven to 500 degrees. Roast meat until skin begins to crisp, approximately 25–30 minutes. Turn oven down to 350 degrees and continue to cook until porchetta reaches a minimum internal temperature of of 160 degrees, approximately 2 hours.

Let rest for 30 minutes and carve.

RYE
WHOLE GRAIN FLOUR
SARTAJ
NO PRESERVATIVES / NO ADDITIVES

Milled & Packaged by : CFP
Tecumseh, Ontario, Canada, (519) 979-1263
www.chanafoodproducts.com
800 g

WHOLE GRAIN DURUM FLOUR
SARTAJ
NO PRESERVATIVES / NO ADDITIVES

Milled & Packaged by : CFP
Tecumseh, Ontario, Canada, (519) 979-1263
www.chanafoodproducts.com
900

HARD RED
WHOLE GRAIN WHEAT FLOUR
SARTAJ
NO PRESERVATIVES / NO ADDITIVES

Milled & Packaged by : CFP
Tecumseh, Ontario, Canada,
www.chanafoodproducts

PURE BESAN (CHICK PEA) FLOUR
SARTAJ
NO PRESERVATIVES / NO ADDITIVES

Milled & Packaged by : CFP
Tecumseh, Ontario, Canada, (519)
oodproducts
900

WHO
S
NO PRES

Milled

SPELT
GRAIN FLOUR
RTAJ
IVES / NO ADDITIVES

by : CFP
(519) 979-1263
oducts.com
900 g

RICE
WHOLE GRAIN FLOUR
SARTAJ
NO PRESERVATIVES / NO ADDITIVES

Milled & Packaged by : CFP
Tecumseh, Ontario, Canada, (519) 979-1263
www.chanafoodproducts.com
900 g

KAMUT
WHOLE GRAIN FLOUR
SARTAJ
NO PRESERVATIVES / NO ADDITIVES

Milled & Packaged by : CFP
Tecumseh, Ontario, Canada, (519) 979-1263
www.chanafoodproducts.com
900

Chana Food Products/ Sartaj Flour

11664 County Road 42, Tecumseh
(519) 979-1263
sartajflour.com

TOOL AND DIE shops are a dime a dozen in Windsor-Essex. Rajason Tools on County Road 42, on the Tecumseh side of the city/county border, is a little different. Through a sister company called Chana Food Products, this plot of industrial land also doubles as a flour mill. And every Friday you can even buy samosas, prepared in a purpose-built industrial kitchen.

That's right: a tool and die shop that sells samosas and grinds flour. It's a combination that could only flourish in diverse and industrial Windsor-Essex. When a colleague first told me about this place, I thought he was pulling my leg.

Rajason Tools traces its roots in Canada to the late 1970s, when a group of brothers from India moved to Windsor. In India, the family had experience producing tractor parts and locomotive steam engines, expertise that they could easily translate to the automotive sector. The business flourished.

That changed in 2008, when the global economy tanked, bringing the auto industry down with it. Looking to diversify, the Chana family decided to turn to another element of their entrepreneurial past: flour. Walk in the front door of the flour mill building today, and you'll find a traditional stone flour mill that was used by the family in India.

Chana's offerings, which are sold under the brand name "Sartaj", are 100% whole grain, certified by the Whole Grains Council. You won't find all-purpose flour here. A more modern stone mill—bigger than the one in the lobby—is used to grind the grains, a process which the family claims produces a better end product due to the lower amount of heat involved.

In addition to wheat, spelt, corn, chickpea, bran and rice flours are sold. The majority of the grains are sourced in Ontario, and as a result, carry the Foodland Ontario logo. It's something you don't see very often, if at all, on the bags of flour sold at the grocery store. In addition

to sales to individuals, Chana's flours are used by some local bakeries and even one large local pizza chain, which uses them for their whole wheat crust.

With the majority of Canada's wheat produced in western Canada, I think it's safe to say that many of us in Ontario—myself included—don't really think a lot about sourcing Ontario-grown, locally-milled flour. However, as the locally-sourced movement grows even stronger, it's nice to know that Windsor-Essex is ahead of the curve.

Corn Flatbread (Mukkhi Roti)

YIELD: 12 FLATBREAD

2 1/4 cups Sartaj whole grain corn flour

1 tsp salt (or to taste)

1/2 tsp black pepper (or to taste)

2-4 fresh green chili peppers (chopped, cayenne pepper can be used as a substitute)

1/2 cup red onion (finely chopped)

1/4 cup fresh cilantro (finely chopped)

1 1/4 cups hot water

1 tbsp ghee or butter (melted)

1 tbsp canola oil

In a medium bowl combine Sartaj whole grain corn flour, salt, and pepper. Add green chilis, onion, and cilantro to the flour mixture.

Drizzle hot water over the mixture, let stand for 2 minutes, stir until the mixture starts to come together, and form a ball.

Turn the dough out onto a lightly floured surface. Gently knead until a soft dough forms (it will still be a little bumpy from the vegetables). Divide the dough into 12 portions and shape each into a ball. Cover with plastic wrap or a slightly damp paper towel.

Fold a large sheet of tinfoil in half lengthwise. Combine ghee (or melted butter) and oil in a small bowl. Place both next to the stove.

Coat a small nonstick skillet with cooking spray and heat over medium heat. Place a ball of dough between sheets of wax paper (leaving the others covered). Press it down to form a patty, then roll it out into a ⅛-inch-thick disc, 4 to 6 inches in diameter (the edges won't be perfectly round and will appear jagged and cracked). Gently peel the dough off the paper and add it to the hot pan. Cook until the underside is light brown in spots, approximately 1–2 minutes. Flip it over and cook for an additional 1–2 minutes. Brush the top with butter-oil mixture and flip it over to sear for 30 seconds. Brush the other side with butter-oil mixture and flip it over to sear for 30 seconds. Slip the bread into the foil sleeve to keep it warm.

Repeat with the remaining dough. Serve warm for breakfast, or with a curry.

Apple Cinnamon Spelt Muffins

YIELD: 8 MUFFINS

1 1/2 cups water
1/2 cup butter
1 1/2 apples cored and shredded
1 cup sugar
2 1/2 tsp cinnamon
1 tbsp vanilla extract
2 cups Sartaj spelt flour
2 tsp baking powder
1 tsp baking soda
1/2 cup raisins (optional)

Mix water, butter, apples, sugar, cinnamon, and vanilla extract in a medium saucepot. Simmer over medium heat for 5 minutes or until mixture begins to thicken.

In a separate bowl, whisk flour, baking powder, and baking soda together. Pour apple mixture into dry ingredients, stir well. Dough will be slightly thick and sticky. Add in raisins.

Divide the mixture into muffin pans and bake at 350 degrees for 30–35 minutes.

Sartaj Chickpea Pasta

YIELD: 1 POUND OF PASTA

4 1/3 cups Sartaj chickpea flour

4 eggs

1 tbsp water (as needed)

Pour flour on counter or board. Make a well in the center. Add one egg at a time. Knead the flour into the eggs. Add the water if needed and knead again until dough is slightly firm. Let rest in a covered bowl in refrigerator for 20 minutes.

If dough is being made for a later date, cover well and keep refrigerated. When ready to use, take out of fridge and allow dough to come to room temperature (approximately 1–2 hours).

Knead dough until it is firm but pliable. Dust counter with flour. Roll dough out to ⅛ inch thickness, dusting with flour as needed, and cut or shape pasta. Allow pasta to dry slightly, approximately 10 minutes.

Boil salted water and add pasta. Toss with your favourite sauce.

Store uncooked pasta in a sealed bag and refrigerate for up to 3 days or freeze for up to 3 months.

Chicken Inn
714 Wyandotte Street East, Windsor
(519) 254-6647
chickeninnrestaurant.com

WINDSOR IS BLESSED with an incredible number of high-quality Middle Eastern restaurants and bakeries, most centered around Wyandotte Street. One of my favourites is Chicken Inn.

I first fell in love with this curiously-named restaurant on the strength of their platters, a fantastic combination that includes some of the best shish tawook, creamchop (fried chicken breast), hummus, and Iraqi-style kabob in the city. In fact, that's all I ever ordered.

It was only when I approached the owners about doing a radio feature that I learned the incredible story of this establishment. Chicken Inn is to Baghdad what Swiss Chalet is to Canada.

Back in Iraq, Hermiz Hermiz owned a factory producing ready-made foods such as meat pies, and a small chain of restaurants serving rotisserie chicken, which, in Arabic, roughly translates to "Chicken Inn". One of the restaurants was located near Baghdad's Firdos Square. That's the place where, in 2003, coalition soldiers famously brought down that massive statue of Saddam Hussein.

A few years before that war broke out, Hermiz sold his businesses, moved his family to Canada and purchased a restaurant in Windsor. Just like in Baghdad, it sold rotisserie chicken.

I'm told that, in Iraq, rotisserie chicken is rather unusual. This is not the case in Canada. With fierce competition, including from some of Canada's biggest supermarkets, Hermiz found it difficult to stand out. So, he started butterflying and charbroiling the chicken and developed a secret sauce that serves as both a marinade and a dipping sauce. Bright and vinegary, the sauce has a hint of heat and a complexity that defies description.

Today, that charbroiled chicken makes up the majority of their sales.

Hermiz sold the business to his sons, Livon and Waleed Mekho, a few years ago. The brothers both have day jobs in information technology, so Hermiz still helps out during the day. Despite the fact that they no longer sell rotisserie chicken, customers from as far as Toronto and Michigan still visit, solely on the strength of Hermiz and the Chicken Inn reputation.

Understandably, Livon and Waleed weren't able to share the recipe to their father's secret chicken for this book. But, as I mentioned, I fell in love with Chicken Inn's other offerings first—and they were more than happy to give some of those recipes to me.

Iraqi Kabobs

YIELD: 4 SERVINGS

3 lbs medium ground beef

2 tbsp salt

1 tbsp black pepper

1/2 lb onion (finely diced)

1 small bunch parsley (finely diced)

Mix beef, salt, pepper, onion and parsley.

Form into small balls and put on skewers.

Grill over medium-high heat until cooked through, approximately 4–5 minutes each side.

Hummus

YIELD: 6 CUPS

2 lbs chick peas (cooked or canned)
1 tbsp salt
1/2 cup tahini
2 tbsp creamy garlic
1/2 cup crushed ice
2/3 cup olive oil
1 tsp red pepper

Mix chickpeas, salt, tahini, garlic, ice, oil, and red pepper in upright mixer until well blended, approximately 5–8 minutes.

Chicken Creamchop

YIELD: 4 SERVINGS

4 6 oz chicken breasts
4 eggs
4 tsp salt
2 tsp pepper
4 cups breadcrumbs
2 cups vegetable oil

Butterfly chicken breasts.

Whisk egg, salt, and pepper together.

Press both sides of chicken into bread-crumbs. Dip in egg wash. Press into bread-crumbs a second time.

Deep-fry each breast for 5–7 minutes. Or, heat vegetable oil in a pan until almost smoking. Fry chicken for about 3–4 minutes, turn and continue cooking until cooked through, approximately 5 minutes.

Fattoush

1 head lettuce (chopped)
1 tomato (diced)
1 1/2 cucumbers (diced)
1 1/2 onions (diced)
1/3 cup olive oil
1/3 cup vinegar
1 tsp sumac
1 tbsp oregano

Mix lettuce, tomato, cucumber, and onions. Toss with oil, vinegar, sumac, and oregano. Serve with fattoush bread.

Cooper's Hawk Vineyards and The Vines Restaurant

1425 Iler Road, Harrow
(519) 738-4295
coopershawkvineyards.com

THE BURGEONING WINE industry in Essex County is a point of pride for me. While the industry has a relatively long history, it's only been over the last decade or so that local wineries have really started to flourish and multiply. One of the most visible of the new harvest, if you will, is Cooper's Hawk Vineyards.

It wasn't supposed to be this way. In fact, Tom O'Brien, the founder of Cooper's Hawk, never intended to start a full-fledged winery. After retiring from a career in finance in 2007, he purchased a farm in Harrow, complete with an agreement to to grow grapes on behalf of a large winery.

Like all good things, grapes take a while to grow. Just as things were getting ready for harvest in 2011, that large winery decided that they didn't need his grapes anymore.

So when life gives you a harvest of grapes, what else can you do but make wine?

Shortly after founding his own winery, Tom became president of EPIC (Essex Pelee Island Coast) Wineries, a trade organization. As a result, he became not just a promoter of his own wine, but of the region as a whole. Since I arrived here in 2012, I've regarded Tom as one of the biggest advocates for the bounty of the region. Incredibly knowledgeable and connected, he's often my first call whenever I have a wine or vineyard-related question.

So when Tom told me that Cooper's Hawk was opening a restaurant, I was delighted. Appropriately called 'The Vines', it opened in

As one would expect for a local winery, local food is the star of the menu, with meats sourced from the Butcher of Kingsville, produce coming from farms such as Lee and Maria's and, of course, fresh perch from Lake Erie. Even the bun for the burger is proudly labelled as coming from Stiemar, an old-school bakery on Ouellette Place known for its equally old-school donuts and traditional breads.

the fall of 2015, and is among the first wineries in the region to have full-service restaurant operating every day of the week.

The man in the kitchen is Michael Boucher. A Red Seal chef who has worked in just about every corner of the province, Michael moved back to Windsor-Essex for his wife, who farms in Colchester.

Much like the winery itself, the food at The Vines is approachable and familiar, yet refined—combining old-school French cooking with modern techniques and international flavours. During a recent conversation, Michael confessed to having a deep love for southern BBQ—in fact, he had recently purchased a smoker.

Wine and southern BBQ? If anybody can pull it off, it's Cooper's Hawk.

Red Wine Vinaigrette

1 cup red wine
1 tbsp sugar
3 sprigs rosemary
1 tbsp Kolzigs rosemary mustard
1 1/2 cups olive oil
salt and pepper
honey (to taste)

In a small saucepan combine wine, sugar, and rosemary. Bring to a simmer and reduce by half.

Remove from heat, cool, and strain to remove rosemary.

Combine the mustard and wine reduction in a bowl. Add oil while whisking slowly. The mixture should emulsify.

Season with salt, pepper, and honey to taste and serve with your favourite salad.

Talon Red Demi-Glace (Liquid Gold)

YIELD: 1 LITRE

1 lb beef soup bones (preferably knuckles)

1 tbsp tomato paste

1/2 cup onion (rough chop)

1/4 cup celery (rough chop)

1/4 cup carrot (rough chop)

1 bottle Talon Red Wine

Roast bones at 450 degrees until they begin to caramelize, approximately 45 minutes.

Apply the tomato paste to the bones and continue to roast until the tomato paste cooks.

Add the onion, celery, and carrot to a large stock pot. Remove the roasted bones from the rendered fat and add the bones to the pot.

Fill the pot with cold water until everything is completely covered. Set over medium-high heat and bring to a slow simmer. Reduce heat and keep at slow simmer for 4 hours.

Strain and return the liquid to the stock pot. Set over high heat and bring to a rolling boil. Reduce until 1 litre of liquid remains. Add the bottle of Talon Red Wine and reduce again to 1 litre or the liquid coats the back of a spoon.

Serve hot over steak or add a tablespoon or two to your beef soup or stew for a richer flavour. Refrigerate for up to two weeks.

Turmeric, Carrot and Riesling Soup

YIELD: 6-8 SERVINGS

1/4 cup butter
1 cup red onion
2 cloves garlic
1 pod cardamom
2 cups Cooper's Hawk Riesling
3 cups carrot
1/2 celery root
1/2 cup celery
1/2 cup leek (white part only)
1 tsp fennel seed (toasted)
5 cups vegetable stock
1/4 bunch dill
salt and pepper

Melt butter in a large pot. Add onion, garlic, cardamom, and sauté to golden brown. Deglaze with 1½ cups of Riesling. Add the carrot, celery root, celery, leek, toasted fennel seed, vegetable stock, and dill. Simmer over medium-high heat for 25–30 minutes.

Purée and pass through a strainer.

Return to a clean pot, add the remaining Riesling, stir, and season with salt and pepper to taste.

Dolan Restaurant

225 Wyandotte Street West #103, Windsor
(519) 997-9850
facebook.com/DolanRestaurant/

WHEN I FIND myself bragging about the diversity of Windsor's food scene with out-of-towners, one of the restaurants I always mention is Dolan. It's one of only a handful of genuine Uyghur (pronounced "WEE-gur") establishments in Ontario—and the fact that Windsor is home to one says a lot about this city.

Uyghurs are a Muslim minority group that live in a politically contested northwestern area of China known as the Xinjiang Uyghur Autonomous Region. There aren't many Uyghurs in Canada, and even fewer in Windsor.

Uyghur restaurants are even rarer.

In fact, shortly after I did my story about the place for CBC, Jennifer Bain, the *Toronto Star*'s food editor at the time, deemed it worthwhile to make the trek to Windsor to do a story about the restaurant. At the time, she said it was only the third authentic Uyghur restaurant in Ontario, the other two being in the greater Toronto area.

The reason I include the word authentic is because, according to Dolan owner Adil Hamit, Uyghur food is incredibly popular in China. In fact, Uyghur food is to the rest of China what "Chinese food" is to North America: ubiquitous. As a result, I'm sure many Chinese restaurants in Ontario serve some Uyghur dishes—but finding a restaurant dedicated to Uyghur food is another story.

Uyghur food reflects the Xinjiang Uyghur Autonomous Region's climate, location and its long historical association with the famed Silk Road; I like to describe it as a hearty blend of Middle Eastern and Chinese ingredients and techniques, with lamb being the protein of choice. At Dolan, the first dish I fell in love with was "laagman"—fresh, hand-pulled noodles stir-fried with vegetables and meat. It's simple, but delicious.

Adil and his family moved to Canada in the late '90s. They settled in the GTA because his mother, a professor of history at Xinjiang University, became a visiting scholar at the University of Toronto. When his parents retired, like many Toronto-area retirees, they moved to Windsor. Adil and his wife Zainura followed a few years later. Opening a Uyghur restaurant had long been a family goal. The attractive cost of doing business in Windsor made it possibile—and so Dolan Restaurant was born in 2013. The entire family is involved. Some of their biggest customers are Chinese students studying at the University of Windsor.

Over the years, I've brought a number of friends and family to the place. One time, a friend who had spent an extensive amount of time in northwestern China paid a visit, excited by the possibility of eating Big Plate Spicy Chicken, a popular dish in Xinjiang Uyghur Autonomous Region. He deemed it just as good—perhaps even better!—than the ones he'd had back in China. This was also the dish the *Toronto Star* waxed poetically about.

I'm a huge fan of the lamb kebabs, a simple but flavourful dish that is bursting with cumin, one of my all-time favourite spices. Due to the fact that making hand-pulled noodles is something that requires a lot of experience, Dolan was gracious enough to share these latter two dishes, which thankfully don't require you to know how to make noodles by hand.

Dolan Lamb Kebabs

YIELD: 4 SKEWERS

2 lbs of boneless lamb leg

2 tsp salt

1 medium onion (diced)

4 tsp cumin

1 tsp dark soy sauce

2 eggs (lightly beaten)

1 cup water

Cut lamb into 1-inch cubes.

In a large bowl or bag mix salt, onion, cumin, dark soy sauce, eggs, and water.

Add lamb and massage until well-coated, then let marinate for approximately 2 hours.

Put onto skewers and grill until they reach a minimum internal temperature of 160.

Big Plate Spicy Chicken

YIELD: 6 SERVINGS

Marinade:

3 cups water

1/4 cup light soy sauce

2 tbsp dark soy sauce

1/2 cinnamon stick

2 whole brown cardamom

2 whole star anise

1 1/2 tsp table or fine sea salt

2 1/2 lb boneless, skinless chicken thighs and/or breasts (cut in 1-inch chunks)

Stir-fry:

1/4 cup canola oil

1 tbsp granulated sugar

1 cup small dried red chili peppers (stemmed, soaked in hot water 15 minutes, drained)

5 large cloves garlic (halved)

12 thin slices peeled ginger

1/2 cup light soy sauce

2 tbsp dark soy sauce

1 lb Yukon Gold or yellow-fleshed potatoes (peeled, chopped in 1-inch chunks)

4 to 6 cups water

1 red or green bell pepper (chopped)

2 jalapeños (chopped)

1 tbsp Chinese broad bean paste with chili

1 tbsp Chinkiang (black rice) vinegar

1 lb dried fettucine (cooked)

Marinade:

In medium saucepan, combine water, light soy, dark soy, cinnamon stick, cardamom, star anise, and salt. Bring to a boil over high heat. Remove from heat and let cool completely.

In sealable plastic bag or covered container, combine chicken and marinade. Refrigerate overnight, turning or stirring occasionally.

Stir-fry:

Heat wok over high heat. Add oil, then sugar. Add chicken. Fry until just cooked through, approximately 7–10 minutes. Add chilies, garlic, and ginger. Fry 2 minutes. Add light and dark soy sauce. Fry 2 minutes. Add potatoes. Fry 2 minutes. Add 4 cups water. Bring to boil, then cover with lid. Cook 10 minutes, adding water as needed. Add bell peppers and jalapeños. Stir in broad bean paste and vinegar. Continue cooking until potatoes are tender, approximately 5 minutes.

Divide noodles among 6 plates or shallow bowls. Using slotted spoon, transfer chicken/potato/vegetable mixture on top of noodles. Using measuring cup, pour generous amount of cooking liquid over each portion.

The Earnest Bagel Company

3041 Dougall Avenue, Unit 4, Windsor
(519) 997-7432
earnestbagel.com

I TRY MY best not to be pretentious when it comes to food. Food doesn't have to be "authentic" to be delicious.

But I draw the line when it comes to bagels.

The bagels you find at most grocery stores, bakeries and coffee shops are not bagels. At best, they're a squishy, flavourless loaf of bread that happens to be formed into a circle.

A proper bagel is crispy on the outside, yet soft and chewy on the inside. A proper bagel is boiled—not steamed—before it is baked. And—I can't believe I have to say this—a proper bagel needs to have a sizeable hole in the middle.

Most importantly, a proper bagel doesn't need to be toasted or sliced; it should have flavour right out of the oven. I'm not saying that you shouldn't use butter or cream cheese; all I'm saying is that you shouldn't have to when it's fresh.

As far as I'm concerned, a North American city is not truly great unless it has a proper bagel shop. That's why the Earnest Bagel Company on Dougall Avenue is so critical to Windsor's culinary fabric.

With a master's degree in public policy and global economy, owner Tristan Fehrenbach isn't your typical bagel maker. He's shaped government policy in Alberta and Ontario. He's travelled the world. And while he'd always wanted to start a business, a bagel shop wasn't the obvious answer.

But in 2010, a few years after returning to Windsor, Tristan found himself eating a proper bagel in Ann Arbor. He wondered why he couldn't get one in Windsor.

After three years of research—including a stint working for the iconic St-Viateur Bagel in Montreal—The Earnest Bagel Company opened in April 2013, selling hand-rolled bagels made in the Montreal-style.

I was highly suspicious. In contrast to their New York cousins, Montreal-style bagels are smaller and denser, with much bigger holes. Most critically, they're sweeter, due to the addition of honey to the boiling bagel water. In my experience, bakeries claiming to sell Montreal-style bagels outside *La Belle Province* are always a disappointment.

The suspicion was misplaced: these bagels were fantastic. Concerned that my memory of Montreal bagels had been compromised, I brought a dozen to a group of ex-pat Montrealers that worked with me at the CBC. They agreed—these were about as close as you could get outside of a ten hour drive up the 401.

I think I ate three of them right out of the bag that first day. Even now, it's rare for a full dozen bagels to make the journey from bakery to home.

For the Montrealers reading this book, I should mention that there is one difference from what you get in Montreal: the size. While not as obese as in New York, these bagels are certainly larger than you might expect. According to Tristan, this is because his dough proofs—or rests—in a chilled environment for at least a day, allowing the bagels to develop a flavour above and beyond what is bestowed from the boiling honey water. It's a technique common for New York-style bagels, but not usually the case in Montreal. I like to think of Tristan's combined New York-Montreal style as a nod to life on the Canada-US border.

Unfortunately, the people at St-Viateur in Montreal swore Tristan to secrecy—so you won't find a recipe for bagels in this book. What you will find, however, is a recipe for his highly sought-after cream cheese, as well as some of his incredible cookies, which I think are almost as good as the bagels.

Cream Cheese Recipes

YIELD: 1 CUP

Green Onion and Garlic Cream Cheese:
1 cup cream cheese
1/2 tsp of garlic powder
1 green onion stalk finely chopped

Stir garlic powder thoroughly into cream cheese. Add green onions. Mix well.

Consider adding any of these flavours:
Chili flakes
Extra virgin olive oil
Walnuts
Chopped kalamata olives

Dill and Lemon Cream Cheese:
1 cup cream cheese
1 tsp freshly squeezed lemon
1 handful of finely chopped fresh dillweed

Mix lemon thoroughly into cream cheese. Add chopped dillweed. Mix well.

Consider adding any of these flavours:
your favourite jam
Nutella
habanero peppers, seeds and all
fresh berries
honey
maple syrup
sun-dried tomatoes

Chocolate Chip Cookies

YIELD: 4-6 DOZEN COOKIES

1 1/4 cups sugar

1 1/4 cups firmly packed brown sugar

1 1/2 cups butter (softened)

2 tsp vanilla

3 eggs

4 1/2 cups all-purpose flour

2 tsp baking soda

1/2 tsp salt

4 cups semi-sweet chocolate chips

Heat oven to 350 degrees.

In a medium bowl beat sugar, brown sugar and butter together until light and fluffy. Add vanilla and eggs; blend well. Mix in flour, baking soda, and salt.

Stir in chocolate chips.

Drop dough by rounded tablespoons 2 inches apart on ungreased cookie sheets.

Bake for 8–10 minutes. Remove and place on rack to cool.

Snickerdoodles

YIELD: 4-6 DOZEN COOKIES

1 cup butter (softened)
1 1/2 cups plus 2 tbsp sugar
2 eggs
2 1/2 cups all-purpose flour
2 tsp cream of tartar
1 tsp baking soda
1/4 tsp salt
2 tbsp sugar
2 tsp cinnamon

Heat oven to 375 degrees.

Cream butter and 1½ cups sugar. Beat in eggs. Mix in the flour, cream of tartar, baking soda, and salt.

Using a tablespoon form 1-inch balls.

Stir 2 tbsp sugar and cinnamon together in a separate dish.

Roll the balls in the sugar mixture. Place on an ungreased cookie sheet.

Bake for 7–8 minutes. Remove and place on rack to cool.

EROS RESTAURAN

OPEN

BUSINESS HOURS

EROS

ASIAN EATERY

怡樂餐廳

519-977-1104

Eros Asian Eatery/ Kagerou Ramen House

2270 Wyandotte Street West, Windsor

(519) 977-1104

facebook.com/ErosAsianEatery/

facebook.com/kagerou.ramen.house/

WYANDOTTE STREET IS my favourite street in the city. It may not have the view of Riverside Drive or the speed of E.C. Row, but what I love about Wyandotte is its varied, urban structure complete with a growing number of bike lanes and relatively frequent transit.

Walkerville and Old Riverside may get all the attention, but if I were to choose a favourite stretch of Wyandotte, the area around the University of Windsor, from Sunset to Campbell, has a feel like no other.

It's the pedestrians.

For the most part, Windsor is a city of wide avenues and underused sidewalks. It wasn't always like this, but the post-war desire to rebuild our environment for the personal automobile has made it this way.

This stretch of Wyandotte breaks that mold. It's narrow. It's noisy. And with the recent streetscape redevelopment project, it's beautiful, with matching street furniture and light fixtures.

Most importantly, it's lined with diverse businesses catering to the people who live and work in the area: students. They're everywhere—walking to class, walking home, jaywalking across the street. I love it.

One of the places where you'll find many of these students is Eros Asian Eatery, located just across the street from the new Ed Lumley Centre of Engineering Innovation. Run by brothers Terry and Solon Wong, Eros started in 1991 when their parents, immigrants from Hong Kong, bought a breakfast place. Over the years, dishes from Hong Kong's cosmopolitan blend of Western and Asian cuisine were added to the menu, and Eros Asian Eatery was born.

A student favourite, the place always seems to be packed. On one visit, I met a customer who drove from Toronto simply to purchase their housemade hot sauce. He'd graduated from the University of Windsor years ago, but his cravings continued.

I first met Terry and Solon when I heard about Eros' Saturday alter-ego, Kagerou Ramen House. A permanent pop-up, Kagerou was the Wongs' way of sharing their love of ramen while ensuring a quality product. Proper ramen is a dish that doesn't lend itself well to being prepared on demand in small quantities—the broth alone takes hours—so offering it only one day a week ensured that they'd do the Japanese classic justice.

It proved so popular that people would line out the door before they opened, and Terry and Solon would run out of ramen hours before they closed. I totally understand it—the ramen is fantastic. These guys did their research, evaluating numerous noodle suppliers and recipes before debuting their dish to the public.

There's obviously demand for ramen in Windsor—and I'm sure they could start serving it every day. Despite this, Kagerou remains a Saturday-only secret.

I actually rather enjoy it this way—absence makes the heart grow fonder, right?

Indonesian Fried Rice

YIELD: 1 SERVINGS

2 tbsp canola oil
6 oz chicken breast (sliced)
6 large shrimp
1/4 tsp of minced garlic
1/4 tsp of minced bird's eye chili
2 eggs
1 1/2 cups of cooked white rice, cooled
1 tsp of salt
2 tbsp of Indonesian sweet soy sauce
1 handful of bean sprouts
6 oz sirloin steak
salt and pepper to taste
2 tbsp of dried shallot

Put 2 tablespoons of canola oil in wok/frying pan and turn heat to medium-high. Stir-fry chicken breast until about half-cooked. Add shrimp and fry until they turn pink. Add minced garlic and chili. Add one egg in the wok along with cooked rice. Stir-fry thoroughly then add a teaspoon of salt followed by a splash of water. Add sweet soy sauce and continue to stir-fry. Put in bean sprouts at the final stage. Try not to overcook the sprouts to preserve crispiness.

Season steak with salt and pepper. Grill or pan-fry to medium rare.

Place fried rice on plate then cook an over-easy fried egg and place on top of the rice. Sprinkle with dried shallot and place steak on the side of the plate.

Thai-Style Stir-Fried Vermicelli with Chicken

YIELD: 2 SERVINGS

16 oz boneless, skinless chicken
   breast

salt and pepper (to taste)

1 tsp sesame seed oil

7 oz dried rice vermicelli

1 tsp Thai-style red curry paste

3 tbsp vegetable oil

1 cup onion (sliced)

1 tbsp sugar

1 tsp fish sauce

2 eggs (beaten)

1 cup bean sprouts

1/2 cup garlic chives (cut into
   2-inch sections)

1/2 cup red peppers (sliced)

1 tsp fried garlic (available at
   Asian grocery stores)

1/2 bunch cilantro (chopped)

1 lime

Cut chicken breast into thin strips, season with salt and pepper, mix in 1 teaspoon of sesame seed oil.

Soak vermicelli in hot tap water for 4–5 minutes, or until noodle is soft but retains a slight bounce.

Break up red chili paste with 1 tablespoon of vegetable oil, mix well.

In a hot wok, add 2 tablespoon of vegetable oil, and stir-fry sliced onion and chicken until chicken is almost cooked. Turn down heat and add red chili paste. Mix well with chicken and onion, then add vermicelli. Stir until vermicelli is evenly coated with paste.

Add sugar and fish sauce, mix well again. Sprinkle water as needed to keep vermicelli soft.

Push vermicelli to the sides of pan to form a well in the middle, turn heat up, and add eggs. Stir eggs until half-cooked, then mix with vermicelli. Add bean sprouts, garlic chives, and red peppers. Fry for an additional 30 seconds.

Transfer to a plate and sprinkle with fried garlic and cilantro. Quarter a lime and put wedges on the side of the vermicelli.

Squeeze lime juice onto vermicelli to taste.

Top: Thai-Style Stir-Fried Vermicelli with Chicken (page 90).
Bottom: Simple Tokyo-Style Shoyu Ramen (page 92).

Simple Tokyo-Style Shoyu Ramen

YIELD: 4 SERVINGS

Chicken Broth:
1 stewing hen
1 small onion (whole)
5-6 slices ginger
6 green onions (washed, root removed)
1 celery stalk

Pork Belly Chashu:
2 lbs slab pork belly
1 cup Japanese soy sauce
1/2 cup sake
4 cups water
1 tbsp brown sugar
2 cloves garlic (crushed)
4-5 slices ginger
2 green onions

Shoyu tare (Soy based seasoning):
1 4 x 5-inch piece of kombu (kelp)
4 cups of water
2 cups of Japanese soy sauce
1/4 cup of mirin (Japanese sweet
    cooking wine)
1/4 cup of Saké
1/4 cup of sugar
2 cups of bonito flakes

Marinated Bamboo Shoot (Menma)
12 dried bamboo shoot slices
1 cup shoyu tare

3 tbsp of sugar
1 cup of water
2 pieces of peeled ginger

4 eggs
ramen noodles (cooked)
2 slices naruto maki fish cake

Chicken Broth:

In a stock pot, cover stewing hen with water, boil for 15–20 minutes. Turn off heat, remove hen from pot and rinse under cold water.

Wash stock pot thoroughly, then cover stewing hen with 6 litres of water, boil, reduce heat and simmer for 4 hours, until the hen begins to fall apart. Add more water as needed. Try not to disturb the hen and break it apart because this will make the stock cloudy. Add onion, ginger, green onion, and celery. Simmer for an additional hour.

Carefully remove the hen and vegetables. Pour stock through a strainer lined with cheesecloth. Cool, and refrigerate overnight. Remove and save the layer of fat at the top of the broth.

Pork Belly Chashu:

Remove skin and excess fat from pork belly and roll into 3–4 inches in diameter and tie with butcher's twine at ½ inch intervals. Sear in a pan.

In small roasting pan, mix soy sauce, Saké, water, and brown sugar. Add pork belly and coat well. Add garlic, ginger, and green onion and cook at

320 degrees for 2½ hours, rotating pork every 30 minutes, coating with liquid, until it reaches an internal temperature of between 160 and 170 degrees. Cool and refrigerate overnight. Strain liquid and set aside.

Shoyu tare:

Soak kombu in warm water in a large sauce pan for an hour, discard kombu. Add bonito flakes, simmer for 5 minutes and discard bonito flakes.

Reduce until there is approximate 3 cups of liquid. Stir in soy sauce, mirin, Saké, and sugar.

Marinated eggs:

Place 4 room-temperature eggs in boiling water for 5 minutes. Put eggs in ice bath for 5 minutes, mark and peel.

Mix one cup of shoyu tare with 2 cups of water and 3 tablespoons of sugar. Place eggs in the mixture and marinate overnight.

Menma (Marinated Bamboo Shoot):

Re-hydrate bamboo shoots in water overnight.

Place ginger slices in a pot of boiling water. Blanch bamboo shoots for 15 minutes then soak in cool water for an hour.

Mix 1 cup of shoyu tare with 2 cups of water and 3 tablespoons of sugar. Marinate bamboo shoots in mixture overnight.

Assembling Ramen:

Over medium-low heat, bring chicken broth to a simmer.

In separate pan, melt chicken fat over low heat, add a slice of ginger and a crushed clove of garlic and cook for 5 minutes.

Boil Chashu liquid and remove from heat. Cut twine from chilled Chashu. Cut Chashu into thin slices. Warm Chashu slices briefly in the liquid. If you have access to a kitchen blow torch, toast Chashu for added colour and flavour.

Cook ramen noodles in a pot of boiling water.

Pour 1½ cups of chicken broth into bowl. Drain cooked noodles well, shake off excess water. Lay cooked noodles into the broth, loosen with a pair of chopsticks.

Arrange chashu, menma, naruto maki, and a marinated egg on top of the noodles. Garnish with finely chopped green onion.

The Fruit Wagon

793 East County Road 50, Harrow /
Downtown Windsor Farmers' Market
(519) 738-4819
facebook.com/thefruitwagon/

I LOVE COUNTY ROAD 50. From the stunning views of Lake Erie to the ample number of wineries—including Oxley Estate (see pages 136-141)—this stretch of road has a lot going for it.

With so much to do on one stretch of road, it can be difficult to narrow down where to stop on a leisurely afternoon drive. Wherever you end up going, one place you can't miss is The Fruit Wagon, a self-serve stand located on the 35 acre Balsillie fruit farm.

Leslie Huffman Balsillie and Doug Balsillie have been farming here—mainland Canada's southernmost fruit farm—since 1981. When they bought the property, it was primarily used to grow peaches. Today, apples are Leslie and Doug's biggest crop, comprising roughly 20 acres. They grow and sell 15 varieties commercially, ending up in places such as the Ontario Food Terminal and eventually, your supermarket.

But Leslie and Doug's interest in apples goes far beyond the selling of established commercial varieties. Their farm is one of 12 test sites in Ontario that grow experimental apples.

Essentially, this means that they're active participants in the search to find the next great apple. When I last spoke to Leslie, they had 10 test varieties on the farm. Some are so new they don't even have names yet—only numbers. While most of us—myself included—may

not be able to tell the difference between these apples and others we might be more familiar with, Leslie can. She has a keen sense of which apple may become the next hit with consumers.

It's not surprising. Until she retired in 2015, Leslie was also employed as the apple specialist in Ontario's Ministry of Agriculture, Food and Rural Affairs (OMAFRA). There's very little she doesn't know about apples—her Twitter handle, @OntAppleLady, is entirely deserved.

So what happens on the remaining acres? Over the years, Doug and Leslie have expanded their operations to a number of other fruits and vegetables, including peaches, plums, berries, cherries, pears (which they also sell commercially), peppers, eggplants, squash, flowers, herbs, and even multiple varieties of kale. Recently, Doug and Leslie added apple cider vinegar—both plain and infused—to their stable of products.

Leslie and Doug were kind enough to share the recipe for their raspberry-cherry pie—a four-time first place winner at the Harrow Fair. In 2016, the pie auctioned for $3200.

And if you're not up for the drive to Harrow to pick up some fruits and veggies, The Fruit Wagon is one of the pillars of the Downtown Windsor Farmers' Market. They're always there, rain or shine.

Raspberry-Cherry Pie

YIELD: 8 SERVINGS

Pie Dough:

2 cups flour

1 cup shortening

4 tbsp water

Filling:

3 cups raspberries

3 cups sour cherries

1 cup sugar

4 tbsp corn starch

2-3 drops almond extract

1 tsp sugar

1 tsp cinnamon

Cut shortening into flour. Stir in water until dough holds together. Divide in half. Roll out to an 11-inch circle about ⅛ inch thick.

Mix raspberries, cherries, sugar, and corn starch until juice forms. Cook in the microwave for 3 minutes, stir well and repeat until it thickens. Add a few drops of almond extract and mix well.

Line a 10-inch buttered pie plate with pastry and pour fruit mixture into pie crust. Top with a lattice of pastry strips and sprinkle top with cinnamon sugar. Bake at 450 degrees for 15 minutes, then turn oven down to 350 degrees for 35 minutes. Cool and serve.

Doug's Appley Burgers

YIELD: 4 SERVINGS

2 lbs ground beef
1 onion (chopped finely)
2 eggs
1 cup oatmeal
1 apple (unpeeled, chopped)
1/2 cup ketchup
1 tbsp Worcestershire sauce
salt
pepper

Mix beef, onion, eggs, oatmeal, apple, ketchup, Worcestershire sauce, salt, and pepper. Divide into 4 balls (approximately 8 oz each). Flatten into patties approximately 1 inch thick.

Grill over medium-high heat for 5–8 minutes on each side. Serve on a bun with your favourite toppings.

Extra burgers can be frozen—layered with wax paper—for up to 3 months.

Hiram Walker & Sons Limited
2072 Riverside Drive East, Windsor
corby.ca

I GREW UP in Peterborough, the long-time home of Quaker Oats' Canadian operations. With a giant plant in centre of the city, the smell of sweet oats, brown sugar and honey defines my childhood memories of the place.

A similar thing has happened in my adopted hometown. The scent I most associate with Windsor is that produced by Hiram Walker, North America's largest alcohol distillery. With a similar grainy note, it could almost be considered the adult evolution of the scent I grew up with.

Contrary to popular belief, this wonderfully yeasty, grainy smell is not caused by the distilling process. Rather, it's generated by the drying grain left over after the beverages are produced. High in protein, this leftover grain is often used as animal feed. With the right wind conditions, you can smell the distillery far beyond Walkerville's boundaries; I sometimes catch its unmistakeable scent at my apartment on Riverside Drive West, which is much closer to that other icon of Windsor, the Ambassador Bridge.

While most people think of Windsor as a town the automobile built, the fact is alcohol came well before Ford and company. Hiram Walker himself was among the first to encourage the establishment of auto manufacturing on this side of the river.

Despite the distillery's rich and long history, I think it's safe to say that the distillery remains a bit of a mystery to those who don't work there. While automotive manufacturing is certainly a much more complex process, I think people—myself included—find it easier to envision what happens inside the plants on Walker Road than they do what happens at Hiram Walker.

Few understand the sheer amount of product that is distilled and bottled in the place. In addition to the Wisers family and most of the Canadian Club portfolio—produced under contract for Suntory, the Japanese company which now owns the rights to the Canadian Club brand—the Walkerville distillery produces myriad other products, including Lamb's Rum, Polar Ice Vodka and McGuinness Liqueurs.

Minivans probably remain Windsor's most valuable export, but I find the fact that Windsor-made booze is sold and consumed around the world pretty incredible.

That's why I was so excited when Don Livermore, Hiram Walker's master blender, agreed to meet and show me around the place for my CBC column. Don has one of the best jobs in Windsor-Essex. With a PhD in brewing and distilling, he's the man who crafts, blends and creates the whiskies I've come to love. And it's not just me who admires his skill—many of his creations, such as the incredible 100% rye Lot 40 and Wisers' Legacy, my personal favourite, have been acclaimed by critics across the county.

Despite its massive size and scale, and the fact that it is owned by Pernod Ricard, the French multinational alcohol corporation, Hiram Walker sourced local ingredients long before it became trendy. Just about all of the corn, rye, wheat and barley—essential ingredients in the making of Canadian whisky—are grown right here in Essex County. From grain to glass, every step of the process happens in Windsor-Essex, with aging taking place in a large facility off Pike Creek in Lakeshore, and bottling occurring back in Windsor on the south side of Riverside Drive. It's an impressive operation that we should be proud to have in our backyard.

You know the phrase, "I wish I could bottle you up and sell it?" In Windsor, it's a reality. The bottle coming out of Hiram Walker are truly a taste of what makes this region great.

Remember the Maine

Glass: Coupe
2 oz Lot No. 40 Rye Whisky
3/4 oz sweet vermouth
1/4 oz cherry liqueur
1 dash Pernod Absinthe
ice
lemon zest

Combine whisky, vermouth, cherry liqueur, and absinthe in mixing glass. Add ice so mixing glass is ¾ full and stir about 15 to 18 times. Strain up in chilled glass. Squeeze a lemon zest across the drink to release the oils, give it a twist and place it in the drink.

J.P. Wiser Float

YIELD: 1 SERVING

Glass: Collins
2 oz J. P. Wiser's Hopped Whisky
2 dashes Angostura bitters
4 oz root beer
1 small scoop of vanilla bean ice cream
ice

Combine whisky and bitters in a glass over ice and then top up with root beer. Stir, then place small scoop of ice cream on top.

Created by Dave Mitton.

Old Pal

Glass: Coupe (up) or Old Fashioned (down)
1 1/2 oz Pike Creek Whisky
3/4 oz dry vermouth
3/4 oz Campari
hard ice
orange zest

Combine whisky, vermouth, and Campari in mixing glass. Add ice so mixing glass is ¾ full and stir about 15 to 18 times. Strain up or over one large cube of ice in glass. Squeeze an orange zest across the drink to release the oils, give it a twist and place it in the drink.

Licia Ruby Food Co.
Various locations in Windsor-Essex
(519) 817-6010
liciaruby.com

I LOVE CHOCOLATE. It's one of the few things that I consistently crave—there's almost always some in the house. And it's not just the high quality stuff I enjoy, either. While there's something to be said for a nice, 70% dark single-origin bar, I'm also just as happy munching on a Cadbury Dairy Milk or a Kit-Kat. Even Neilson chocolate macaroons have a place in my heart.

White chocolate is a different story. It's far too sweet, with little flavour except vanilla. So when I saw a booth at the Walkerville Night Market offering "roasted white chocolate", I didn't know what to expect.

They were handing out free samples, so I took one. It was nothing like the white chocolate to which I was accustomed. It was airy, like an Aero Bar, but with notes of caramel, toffee and fudge.

The man behind the roasted white chocolate was Johnny Oran. He runs Licia Ruby Food Co., which he owns with his wife, Elise. The company gets its name from his two grandmothers. Born and raised in Windsor, Johnny is a Stratford-educated chef who has worked all over the country, including such places as BC's Okanagan valley and Montreal. He even had a stint farming near my hometown of Peterborough.

Most impressively, Johnny spent nearly a year working at Toronto's Splendido, a now-shuttered fine dining restaurant that was considered by many to be among that city's best. Though I certainly didn't have the money to go frequently, Splendido was a place I would save up to celebrate special occasions at when I lived in the greater Toronto area. It remains the standard by which I judge all fancy restaurants.

Like many young people who leave Windsor-Essex, Johnny and Elise—who also trained as a chef—moved back to Windsor in 2012 to raise their family. Working at a number of restaurants, including a large golf course, Johnny noticed that one of his most popular desserts involved the use of roasted white chocolate. Requiring in-house preparation, roasted white chocolate can be quite brittle, and is therefore usually served in bark or as a topping, or even melted into sauce. Johnny would serve it as a *petit-four* at the end of a meal. Customers would visit his restaurants just for the roasted white chocolate.

When Johnny tired of restaurant life, he figured that roasted white chocolate would make a delicious signature product for a food company. After perfecting the process of making roasted white chocolate bars, Licia Ruby was born in the summer of 2015.

While the company is best known for their chocolate, Licia Ruby is also one of the region's most interesting small-scale caterers and market vendors. Hosting pop-up dinners for the public, private parties and interesting, hard-to-find prepared foods at local markets, the presence of such an enterprise speaks volumes to the strength and diversity of the food scene in Windsor-Essex.

Rhubarb, Elder Flower and Roasted White Chocolate Pavlova

YIELD: 4-6 SERVINGS

1/2 cup freeze-dried strawberries

Meringue:
1 1/4 cups of sugar
1 tbsp of cornstarch
1/2 cup of egg whites
1 tbsp of white vinegar

4 to 6 stalks of rhubarb
fresh elder flowers (cut from the stems just before plating)
1 Licia Ruby roasted white chocolate bar
4 cups water
2 cups sugar

Roasted white chocolate Chantilly:
1 1/4 cups of 35% cream
1 tbsp of honey
2 Licia Ruby roasted white chocolate bars (broken into rough pieces)
1 tsp of orange blossom water

Place 1/2 cup of freeze-dried strawberries into a spice grinder and make into a powder.

Meringue:
Mix sugar and cornstarch together until there are no clumps. Heat oven to 225 degrees. Line a baking sheet with parchment paper. In an upright mixer with the whisk attachment add egg white and begin whisking on medium. As soon as eggs begin to froth add ¼ cup of sugar mixture and whisk for 1½ minutes, then add another 1/4 cup of sugar mixture and repeat this process until all of the sugar has been added. Add white vinegar and continue to mix until meringue is shiny and forms stiff peaks. Once the meringue is finished take a large spoon and scoop nice heaping mounds onto the baking tray. Place hot water into a cup and dip a large spoon into the hot water. Take the back of the spoon and make a shallow hole in the center of each cloud. Bake for 1½–2 hours until meringue is dried through.

Rhubarb:
Cut stalks into 6-inch long strips. In a medium saucepan over medium heat mix 4 cups of water and 2 cups of sugar and bring to a simmer, mixing until all the sugar has dissolved. Reduce heat to medium-low and add rhubarb stalks. Simmer 4–5 minutes, then gently flip over and poach the other side for 4–5 minutes, or until you can put a toothpick through the stalk with very little resistance. Using a slotted spatula, remove rhubarb and reserve on a plate lined with plastic wrap and keep in fridge.

Roasted white chocolate Chantilly:
Place cream and honey in a small saucepot and bring to a light simmer. While cream is heating place white chocolate in a heat-proof bowl. Pour cream over the white chocolate and let sit for 1 minute. Add orange blossom water and

whisk cream and chocolate together until all the chocolate is dissolved and there are no lumps. Place the cream mixture in a container and lay some plastic wrap on top of the liquid so that no skin forms on the top. Place in fridge until cool.

Plating the dessert:
Put the roasted white chocolate chantilly into an upright mixer and whisk for 2–3 minutes on medium speed until soft peaks are formed.

Place dried meringue clouds on the plates. Cut each rhubarb stalk in half and place 3 pieces of rhubarb in the center of each cloud. Put a large spoonful of the roasted white chocolate chantilly on top of the rhubarb. Using a fine strainer sift freeze-dried strawberry powder on top of the plates.

Garnish with elder flowers.

Rosemary-Marinated Lamb Saddle with Garlic Sourdough, Mushroom Ragu and Mountainoak Gouda

YIELD: 4 SERVINGS

2 lbs lamb saddle or rack of lamb

1 3/4 cup rosemary olive oil

6 cloves garlic (crushed)

1 pint chanterelle mushrooms (halved)

1 pint shiitake mushrooms (halved)

2 pints oyster mushrooms (halved)

1 pint button mushrooms (halved)

1/4 cup garlic oil

1 pinch kosher salt

3 tbsp butter

1 cup of pomegranate quince balsamic

1/4 cup water

3 pinches salt

1/2 cup golden raisins

1 loaf sourdough bread

olive oil

truffle oil

Mountainoak Wild Nettle gouda

basil pesto

Marinate lamb in 1 cup rosemary olive oil and garlic for 12–24 hours. Half an hour before cooking pull lamb from fridge and let it come to room temperature.

Sauté all mushrooms over medium-high heat with ¼ cup rosemary olive oil and ¼ cup garlic oil. Season with kosher salt, tossing until mushrooms are evenly cooked. Add 3 tablespoons of butter to pan. Set aside.

Over medium heat simmer 1 cup of pomegranate quince balsamic with ¼ cup of water and 2 pinches of salt. Add ½ cup of golden raisins to the balsamic and simmer for 2–3 minutes until raisins are re-hydrated.

Remove lamb from marinade and generously season all sides of the lamb with salt. Heat ½ cup rosemary oil in a pan over medium-high heat. Sear all sides of the lamb.

Remove from pan and place on a baking rack and cook in oven at 375 degrees for 6–12 minutes, depending on your personal preference.

Place 1-inch thick slices of sourdough bread—tossed in olive oil—in the pan the lamb was seared in over medium-low heat and toast both sides of the bread until nice and golden. Season both sides of bread with a pinch of salt.

In a separate pan sauté mushrooms, tossing till hot throughout.

Remove lamb from the oven and let it rest a few minutes.

Place toasted sourdough on a plate, and top with mushrooms and some of the liquid in the pan, allowing the mushrooms to fall off the bread. Take each portion of lamb and slice through the middle at an angle. Place the lamb next to the bread. Drizzle truffle oil over lamb and mushrooms. Place 1 tablespoon of pickled raisins around the lamb and finish with grated wild nettle gouda and basil pesto.

Little Foot Foods

Delivery and various locations in Windsor-Essex
(226) 246-2382
littlefootfoods.com

YOU'D NEVER EXPECT it from the outside, but the Riverside Sports Centre on a quiet stretch of Ontario Street is the headquarters of a burgeoning comfort food empire.

Founded in 2013, Little Foot Foods delivers ready-to-heat foods to homes across Windsor and Essex County. The brainchild of Rachael Myers and her husband, Rob, the idea for the business came when Rachel finished up a master's degree in political science at the University of Windsor. The thought of spending the rest of her life working in an office held no appeal—so she decided that she needed to do something else for a living.

So she turned to her other expertise—something she learned not at school, but from her Polish grandmother: perogies. What makes Rachael's family recipe special is that it calls for an ultra-thin pastry, allowing for a high filling-to-dough ratio. The result is a fast-cooking, wonderfully flavourful perogie—perfect for freezing and heating at home.

Little Foot Foods—which gets its name from the idea of using as many local ingredients as possible, to lower its carbon footprint—offers over a dozen fillings, from the standard onion or sauerkraut to more creative items like habanero cheddar or savoury sage. A selection of seasonally-available "pie"rogies are also sold.

Twice a week, perogies and other comfort foods such as cabbage rolls, savoury biscuits and cookies make their way from the modest commercial kitchen at the Riverside Sports Centre to homes across Windsor and Essex County. Limited edition flavours are also produced in conjunction with other food purveyors. The award-winning chorizo from Robbie's Gourmet Sausage Co. (see pages 160–165), for example, is combined with egg and cheese to create a breakfast perogie you can find in his store's freezer. A series of collaborations with The Willistead (see pages 166–171) resulted in a perogie filled with kangaroo meat for a wild game dinner.

Understandably, Rachael and Rob were hesitant to give up their secret perogie recipe for the book. It's not that the ingredients are particularly exotic; it's the technique that makes it special. I did, however, convince them to part with some of their other fantastic comfort foods. And if you're looking for perogie, flip over to my entry on the legendary Ukrainian Restaurant (see pages 184–189).

Stuffed Jumbo Shells

YIELD: 30 SHELLS

30 jumbo shell noodles
2 tbsp oil
1 medium onion (diced)
4 cloves garlic (minced)
1 bag baby spinach
1 tsp nutmeg
1 1/2 cups parmesan
1 cup ricotta
2 eggs
2 tbsp heavy cream
2 28oz can tomatoes
1 carrot (chopped)
1 celery (chopped)
1 pinch bay leaves
2 tsp oregano
2 tsp rosemary
2 tbsp butter
2 tsp salt
1 tsp pepper
1 tbsp sugar
1 tsp red pepper flakes

In a large pot, boil 2 litres of water and cook jumbo shell noodles until al dente, approximately 7–9 minutes. Drain and cool in cold water. Drain again.

Heat oil in frying pan, add half the onion, and garlic, sauté for 5 minutes. Add washed baby spinach, cover and, stirring occasionally, cook until spinach is wilted, approximately 2 minutes. Remove from heat, stir in nutmeg, 1 cup parmesan and ricotta. Add eggs and cream and stir until a thick paste forms.

In a saucepot combine tomatoes (with liquid), carrot, celery, bay leaves, oregano, rosemary, butter, ½ cup parmesan, salt, pepper, sugar, and red pepper flakes. Simmer for an hour. Press sauce through a strainer to remove bay leaves and any larger vegetable pieces.

Stuff shells with spinach and cheese mixture.

Cover bottom of baking dish with sauce. Add stuffed shells and cover with sauce. Sprinkle with parmesan and bake at 375 degrees for 35–40 minutes, or until cheese is golden brown.

Blue Cheese Biscuits

YIELD: 9 BISCUITS

3 cups all-purpose flour
1 tsp salt
1/2 tsp baking soda
2 tsp baking powder
1 3/4 cups blue cheese
3/4 cup butter
1 cup buttermilk

Combine flour, salt, baking soda, and baking powder.

Grate blue cheese and dice butter.

Combine flour mix with 1 cup cheese and ½ cup butter, should form a fine crumble consistency (rough sand). Add buttermilk, mix until just combined.

Turn out onto table and knead until dough forms. Press dough into a flat circle. Cut out biscuits using cookie cutter. Roll biscuits into balls, cut into quarters. Cover bottom of pie plate with ¼ cup butter and ¾ cup blue cheese. Place biscuits in pan and bake at 375 degrees for 20–25 minutes.

Carrot Cake

YIELD: 16 SERVINGS

1 1/2 cups all-purpose flour

1 1/4 cups sugar

2 tsp baking soda

2 tsp cinnamon

1 tsp salt

1 tsp nutmeg

1 medium carrot

2/3 cup oil

2 eggs

1 tsp vanilla

1 cup finely diced pineapple

3/4 cup raisins

1/2 cup crushed walnuts

1 cup cream cheese (softened)

1/4 cup butter (softened)

1 tsp vanilla extract

1 cup icing sugar

In a large bowl combine flour, sugar, baking soda, cinnamon, salt, and nutmeg. Grate carrot, and add to flour mix.

In separate bowl combine oil, eggs, and vanilla. Stir into flour mixture.

Mix in pineapple, raisins, and walnuts.

Pour into 9 x 13 baking dish and bake at 350 degrees for 40–45 minutes. Cool.

Mix cream cheese, butter, and vanilla with wooden spoon until smooth. Add icing sugar, continue stirring until fully incorporated.

Once the cake has cooled spread icing evenly over cake.

The Little White Kitchen Baking Co.

543 Lincoln Road, Windsor
(519) 915-5554
facebook.com/thelittlewhitekitchenbakingco/

EVERY TIME I walk into the Little White Kitchen Baking Co. in Walkerville, I register a complaint with the owner, Michele Bowman.

"Listen Michele," I say. "Can you please stop making delicious items? Or, at the very least, can you stop taking beautiful pictures of them?"

Michele usually laughs and hands me whatever wonderful creation I've ordered. Maybe it's a croissant. Or perhaps her interpretation of Australia's iconic Tim Tam. Or a gargantuan, incredibly decadent cinnamon bun.

Multiple times a day, my Instagram feed is filled with drool-worthy pictures of the latest and greatest food coming out of the Lincoln Road bakery. When Michele first opened, I was stopping by multiple times a week to munch on her latest creation. If it wasn't for the threat of an enormously expanding waistline, I'd probably drop by every day. She's just that good.

A professional photographer before she got into baking, Michele Bowman is the perfect food entrepreneur for today's social media-centred world, combining my generation's love for food with our even greater desire to document it. What makes The Little White Kitchen particularly great is that her pictures are truth in advertising: the product is really as good as it looks.

I first met Michele when she was turning her personal food blog into a small home-based bakery, selling at the Downtown Windsor Farmers' Market and other local events. At the time, she

specialized in gluten-free products, due to the fact that her daughter is gluten intolerant.

What surprised me most was that I found it incredibly hard to tell which of her goods were gluten-free; they were as good as those which weren't! Her ice-cream sandwiches were a particular favourite, combining incredibly decadent, homemade ice cream—frozen custard, really—with huge, wonderfully chewy cookies.

Gluten-free or not, these were the best ice-cream sandwiches I'd had—anywhere. I wasn't alone. People came to the Saturday market with cooler bags to stock up. Local restaurants started selling them as desserts.

After two successful seasons at the market, Michele quit the photography business and pursued baking (and ice-cream sandwiches) full-time. After a lengthy build-out that even involved a change of location, The Little White Kitchen Baking Co. opened in August 2015 in a former cabinet factory. It serves both gluten-free and gluten-full items, along with bakery-style lunch, coffee and tea. Having amassed a huge following at the market and through social media, the line-ups started on the very first day.

When I'm showing visitors the city for the first time, the Little White Kitchen is often my first stop. Located right beside the popular City Cyclery, the Little White Kitchen is a glimpse into the type of vibrant, successful urban place Windsor can be. Her business is proof that you don't need a massive parking lot or visibility from a major thoroughfare to get customers. Through the power of social media savvy and incredible baking talent, Michele and her staff have attracted customers from all over the city, county and even across the border.

Apple Pie Cake

Caramel Sauce:

3/4 cup whipping cream

1/2 cup sugar

2 tbsp water

1 tsp honey or corn syrup

1/2 tsp salt

4 tbsp unsalted butter, softened

1 tsp vanilla

Candied Pecans:

1/3 cup white sugar

pinch of cinnamon

1 tbsp water

2/3 cup pecan halves

Cake:

2 cups all-purpose flour

1/2 tsp salt

6 tsp ground cinnamon

4 tsp baking powder

2 1/3 cups white sugar

4 eggs

1 cup vegetable oil

2 tsp vanilla extract

6 apples (peeled, cored, and sliced thinly)

1 cup toasted pecans, chopped

Caramel Sauce:

In a small bowl, microwave the whipping cream on high for 1 minute, set aside.

In a medium saucepan, gently mix the sugar, water, honey, and salt. Do not stir again. Turn heat up to medium-high, bring the sugar to a boil until it reaches a medium/dark amber colour. During the cooking, wipe down the inside of the pot with a wet pastry brush if sugar crystals start to form on the sides. Once the desired colour is reached, remove from heat and slowly pour in the whipping cream, being careful to avoid the steam (it will bubble up violently). Add soft butter and stir until well-blended. Mix in vanilla and set aside to cool.

Candied Pecans:

In a small frying pan, mix together sugar, cinnamon, water, and pecans. Cook over medium-high heat. The sugar will first melt and then start to crystallize.

Once all the moisture is gone and the nuts are coated in sugar crystals, remove from heat and spread the nuts on a baking sheet to cool.

Cake:

Heat oven to 350 degrees. Grease a 10-inch springform pan.

In a small bowl, blend together the flour, salt, 4 teaspoons cinnamon, and baking powder.

In another small bowl, mix together ⅓ cup sugar and 2 teaspoons cinnamon. Set aside.

The Little White Kitchen Baking Co.   119

In an upright mixer, beat eggs and 2 cups sugar for 5 minutes on high, or until thick and light in colour. Blend in the oil and vanilla. Slowly add the dry ingredients and beat until well-blended.

Mix apples with nuts and toss in cinnamon sugar.

Stir apples and nuts into the cake mixture. Pour into a springform pan and bake for 80–90 minutes, or until a toothpick comes out of the centre clean. Remove from oven and cool. Drizzle with caramel sauce and candied pecans for serving.

Chocolate-Dipped Caramel Swirl Classic Vanilla Marshmallows

YIELD: 12 SERVINGS

Caramel swirl:

1/3 cup sugar

2 tbsp water

1 tsp corn syrup

3 tbsp heavy cream

1 pinch salt

Coating :

3/4 cup icing sugar

1/2 cup cornstarch

Toffee:

1/2 lb butter

1 cup white sugar

1/4 cup water

1 tbsp corn syrup

1 cup pecans, finely chopped

1 pinch salt

Marshmallows:

4 1/2 tsp unflavored powdered gelatin (or 2 packages of Knox gelatin)

3/4 cup cold water

3/4 cup granulated sugar

1/2 cup light corn syrup

1/8 tsp fine salt

2 tsp pure vanilla extract

Caramel:

Stir together sugar, water, and corn syrup in a small saucepan over high heat. Stir until the sugar is dissolved and the mixture starts to boil. Do not stir anymore, but gently tilt the pot to one side to distribute the cooking caramel. When the caramel reaches a dark amber colour, remove from heat and add cream. Whisk, and add salt. Set aside in a medium bowl.

Coating:

Sift together the cornstarch and the icing sugar in a medium bowl. Set aside.

Homemade Butter Toffee:

Place the butter, sugar, water, and corn syrup in a medium saucepan. With the pot over medium-high heat, stir constantly until the mixture boils and the sugar is dissolved. Turn down to medium heat and cook until the mixture reaches 300 degrees, stirring occasionally with a wooden spoon. Do not over-stir.

Remove from heat, pour in the pecans and the pinch of salt.

Spread the hot toffee onto a baking sheet lined with parchment paper and allow to cool on a baking rack. Once cooled, break into pieces and place in a Ziploc bag. Seal the bag and break toffee into small bits with a rolling pin.

Marshmallows:

Pour gelatin into ½ cup water in a microwave-safe bowl and let it sit for 5 minutes, until soft. In a medium saucepan, over high heat, stir together sugar, ¼ cup of corn syrup, ¼ cup of water, and salt. Bring to a boil, stirring occasionally, until the temperature reaches 240 degrees.

Pour ¼ cup of corn syrup into the bowl of an upright mixer fitted with a whisk attachment. Microwave the gelatin on high until completely melted, approximately 30 seconds. Pour into mixer bowl, turn to low and leave it running.

Slowly pour sugar syrup into the bowl (the mixer should still be running). Increase the speed to medium and whip for 5 minutes. Increase the speed to medium-high and whip 5 additional minutes. Add vanilla, increase speed to the highest setting, and whip until opaque white, fluffy, and tripled in volume, approximately 1–2 minutes.

Working quickly, scoop out about a quarter of the marshmallow mixture into the bowl containing the caramel. Whisk mixture together until well-blended. Scrape the caramel marshmallow back into the bowl with the remaining vanilla marshmallow and with a large spatula make big figure eights movements to gently swirl the two, making sure to leave large ribbons of caramel.

Pour the marshmallow mixture into a greased 8 x 8 baking pan and use an offset spatula to smooth it into the corners. Sift ½ cup of the coating evenly and generously over top. Let the marshmallow sit uncovered for at least 6 hours in a cool, dry place.

Use a knife to loosen the marshmallow slab from the edges of the pan. Dust a work surface with a thin layer of the reserved coating. Invert the marshmallow slab onto the work surface and dust it with more coating. Cut into squares. Dip the sticky edges of the marshmallows in the remaining coating, patting off the excess. Store in an air-tight container at room temperature for up to 1 month.

Dipping-in Chocolate:

In a bowl placed over a pot containing simmering water, place ¾ of the chocolate pieces and stir until melted and smooth. Remove the bowl from the heat and add the remaining chocolate. Stir until all the chocolate is melted together.

With a fork, dip each piece of marshmallow into the chocolate, coat all sides and gently tap the fork on the edge of the bowl to remove any excess. Place the dipped marshmallow onto a baking sheet lined with parchment paper. Sprinkle with butter toffee.

Allow chocolate to set.

Store the dipped marshmallows in an air-tight container for up to 1 week.

Mamo Burger Bar

1515 Ottawa Street, Windsor /
3430 Tecumseh Road East, Tecumseh
519-973-1234 / 519-735-3999
mamoburgerbar.com

WHEN I MOVED to Windsor, 1515 Ottawa Street was the home of Sweet T's Soul Cookin', Chef Ryan Odette's chicken-focused replacement for Smoke & Spice, a southern-style barbecue joint that he moved to a larger venue on Tecumseh Road. Fried chicken is a particular favourite of mine—and Sweet T's did it well. They even served chicken and waffles, a dish almost impossible to find on this side of the Detroit River.

So when I heard that Ryan was shutting down Sweet T's and replacing it with a burger joint, I won't lie: I was initially disappointed. As far as I was concerned, good gourmet burgers weren't that hard to find in Windsor. I also thought it a trend which was past its best-before date.

But because I respected Ryan's skills as a chef, I paid a visit to Mamo Burger shortly after it opened in 2013. I was hooked. I became a born-again burger believer.

One of the major issues I have with most gourmet burger joints is how little attention is paid to the patty. A place may have great buns and a plethora of toppings and condiments, but the meat of the matter is often unremarkable. While most places make their own patties, they either use too much lean beef or the final product is often so overcooked that excessive use of sauces and toppings is absolutely necessary.

Mamo's patties, on the other hand, are juicy and flavourful. A lot of this has to do with the fact that they're cooked on a griddle, not a grill—which locks in the fat. Let's face it: burgers are not health food, so the fattier, the better.

But a focus on good patties doesn't mean that the toppings are an afterthought. Mamo's signature burgers may look overwhelming, but they're well-considered, with an excellent balance of flavours. My go-to burger is the "Big Popper", a wonderful balance of beef, heat and creamy, fried goat cheese. It's spicy, decadent, insanely addictive—and, I'm happy to write, one of the recipes Ryan was kind enough to share.

Big Popper

1 7 oz can chipotles in adobo sauce
4 cups mayonnaise
6 oz goat cheese
2 eggs
1 cup milk
1 cup flour (for dredging)
2 cups panko breadcrumbs
4 whole jalapeño peppers
canola oil
kosher salt
2 lbs medium ground beef
8 slices bacon
8 slices hot pepper colby cheese
4 brioche-style burger buns

Combine chipotles in adobo with mayonnaise in a food processor. Purée. Set aside.

Crumble goat cheese, roll into 4 evenly-sized balls. With a plate and parchment paper, press into thin pucks. Refrigerate for at least 15 minutes.

Prepare egg wash by whisking eggs and milk thoroughly. Dust goat cheese pucks with flour, dip in egg wash and then in panko breadcrumbs, then dip in egg wash and panko a second time. Set aside.

Rinse off jalapeños and place on oven-proof pan. Drizzle with oil and season with salt. With your hands, evenly distribute salt and oil all over peppers. Roast at 350 degrees

for 20 minutes. Cool. Remove stem from peppers, slice lengthwise and remove seeds.

Divide beef into 8 evenly-sized balls, and—between two pieces of parchment paper—press them down with a plate to form thin beef patties.

In a skillet over medium-high heat cook bacon. Remove excess fat. Set aside. Season burger patties with kosher salt and cook, using the same pan, for 4–5 minutes on one side. Flip, continue cooking for 3 minutes, and place colby cheese slice on top of all cooked patties. Set aside. Remove pan from heat and put roasted jalapeños in to warm.

Heat deep fryer to 375 degrees. Cook goat cheese puck for 90 seconds. Set aside on paper towel to remove excess oil. If using a skillet, over medium-high heat, add 1/4 cup of vegetable oil, heat until almost smoking. Gently place breaded goat cheese in oil, cook for 45 seconds, until golden brown on both sides. Pat with a paper towel to remove excess oil.

Lightly toast the bun in an oven, grill, or skillet. Spread the top halves of the bun with chipotle mayonnaise. Top each bottom with, in order: 2 beef patties, bacon, roasted jalapeños and fried goat cheese. Add the top bun.

Peanut Butter Jelly Time

YIELD: 1 SERVING

1/4 cup strawberry jelly

1 tbsp sriracha

8 oz fresh ground beef

kosher salt

2 slices of cooked bacon

1 tbsp creamy peanut butter

4 slices dill pickles

6 slices pickled jalapeños

1 hamburger bun

Mix strawberry jelly and sriracha together in a small bowl. Set aside.

Divide beef into two, form into patties and season with kosher salt. Cook until no longer pink in a cast-iron skillet, approximately 4–5 minutes each side. Spread peanut butter on bottom of toasted bun. Place burger patties on bottom hamburger bun and top with pickles, jalapeños, bacon strips, and sriracha jelly.

The Italian Job

1 red onion (sliced thin)
1/4 cup red wine vinegar
1/4 cup sugar
1/2 cup mayonnaise
1/4 cup roasted garlic
1 bunch basil
8 oz fresh ground beef
kosher salt
2 slices mozzarella cheese
2 slices tomatoe
1 slice prosciutto
3 slices salami
1 hamburger bun

Place red onions in a heat-proof bowl, bring sugar and red wine vinegar to a boil in a medium saucepan and pour over red onions and cool to room temperature. Cover and marinate onions for at least 12 hours.

Purée mayonnaise, roasted garlic, and basil in a food processor or blender until fully mixed.

Make two 4oz burger patties with ground beef and season with kosher salt. Cook until no longer pink in a cast-iron skillet, approximately 4–5 minutes each side. Melt 1 slice of cheese on each patty. Place patties on toasted hamburger bun then layer with salami, prosciutto, pickled red onions, tomatoes, and basil mayo.

Nico Ristorante

851 Erie Street East, Windsor
(519) 255-7548
nicoristorante.com

VIA ITALIA, THE HEART of Windsor's Italian community, is one of this city's most beloved neighbourhoods. Home to a number of Windsor's best restaurants, I don't think it's a stretch to say that at least one Erie Street eatery is guaranteed to be on every Windsorite's list of places to eat. Nico Ristorante is the place on my list—and I'm not alone.

Whenever I pass the tiny establishment on the southeast corner of Erie and Elsmere, it always seems to be packed. Sometimes there's a sign on the door telling diners they're out of luck if they don't have a reservation. Even on days where the rest of the street is dead, Nico always seems to have people inside.

When I last visited, there were even a number of American diners—a much rarer breed these days. While I'm told the American presence is not like it was in the heyday of the 1990s, Nico, at least, is noticing an uptick.

Nico Ristorante opened in 1997 and is owned by chef Nick Politi. The name is a homage to his grandparents: incredibly, both sets were named Nicola and Nicoletta. I first heard about the place not online or from loyal customers, but from people who work in Windsor's culinary industry. It makes sense—a number of Windsor's most talented chefs, including Rino Bortolin, got their start under Nick.

I think the key to what makes Nico so successful is the fact that the menu changes frequently—three times a week. In addition, compared with some other restaurants in the area, the menu is tiny, with only a handful of entrees and fresh-made pastas available at any one time. Most notably, this isn't a place where you'll find many Italian-American mainstays like fettucine alfredo or chicken parmigiana.

Don't get me wrong—there's nothing wrong with Italian-American cuisine. I love chicken and veal parmigiana, and Windsor-style pizza is my favourite kind of pie, despite the fact that it would likely be unrecognizable to an Italian. But you can find these dishes at other places.

I think what brings people back to Nico time and time again is the fact that its offerings are unique. Many of the dishes on the menu are not well-known in North America. Nick makes extensive use of less popular meats such as tripe, salt cod and wild boar, sometimes in the same dish. His wild boar bolognese, for example, uses chicken livers, pancetta and sausage in addition to the boar.

When I asked Nick what drives his menu, the answer was simple. "I make dishes that I want to eat," he said. It's a good philosophy.

Cioppino or Ligurian Seafood Stew

YIELD: 4-6 SERVINGS

2 tbsp olive oil

1 small onion (small to medium dice)

1 green pepper (small to medium dice)

2 celery stalks (small to medium dice)

2 cloves garlic (small diced)

1/2 cup chopped bacon, pancetta or quanciale (optional)

1 lb scrubbed and rinsed fresh clams (Littleneck, pasta clams, Quahogs or Manilla)

1/2 litre peeled crushed or chopped tomatoes in their juice

2 cups white wine

1 cup clam juice

1 pound rinsed mussels (discard open ones that don't close when you tap them)

1 pound of either 16/20 size shrimp or large sea scallops or a combination of both

1 to 2 pounds of (one or a combination of) cod, halibut, chilean sea bass, salmon, red snapper, etc. (boneless, skinless and cut into large 1-inch dice)

salt (to taste)

dried chili flakes (to taste)

chopped parsley (to taste)

basil (to taste)

In a large stock pot sauté onion, pepper, celery, garlic and pork in olive oil over medium heat until vegetables start to soften, approximately 3–5 minutes.

Add the fresh clams and sauté for an additional five minutes. Add tomatoes, wine and clam juice. Raise the heat to high and cover pot. Cook for approximately 5 minutes, until the clams begin to open.

Add mussels and remaining seafood, season with salt to taste and lower heat to medium. Simmer gently until fish is cooked and mussels and clams have opened up. Discard any that haven't.

Add salt, dried chili flakes, chopped parsley, and basil.

Ladle into bowls over about 3 or 4 ounces of your favourite cut of pasta or serve as a soup with garlic bread.

* One of the best places for seafood in Windsor is Mediterranean Seafood, just a few blocks away from Nico at Parent.

Duck Marsala (Anatra alla Marsala)

YIELD: 4 SERVINGS

4 duck legs (with thigh attached)

salt and pepper to taste

1 small red onion (diced)

2 medium carrots (diced)

2 celery stalks diced

1 whole garlic bulb split into separate cloves but not peeled

1/2 bottle sweet Marsala wine

4 cups chicken or beef stock

2 tbsp brown sugar

3 or 4 sprigs thyme

Pre-heat oven to 400 degrees. Pat duck legs dry and season with salt and pepper.

Heat a large sauté pan on high and brown the duck legs on all sides. Reduce heat to medium after a few minutes so you don't burn the duck.

Transfer the legs to a plate and cook the vegetables over medium heat in the remaining duck fat, including the unpeeled garlic. Transfer to roasting pan and add Marsala, stock, brown sugar, thyme and browned duck legs. Cook covered for 45 minutes at 300 degrees. Remove cover and cook an additional 30–40 minutes.

The duck is ready when the meat is very tender and can be pulled off easily with a fork. If liquid is too watery, reduce in a pan or pot over high heat until it's thick enough to coat the duck (but not syrupy).

Wild Boar Bolognese

YIELD: 4-6 SERVINGS

2 tbsp olive oil

1/2 lb slab bacon or pancetta (ground or finely chopped)

2 lbs ground wild boar

1/2 lb mild sausage

3 tsp salt

1 medium onion (diced)

4 stalks celery (diced)

4 carrots (diced)

1 6oz can tomato paste

2 cups whole milk

1 cup dry white wine

1 cup chicken or beef stock

8 oz chicken livers (puréed with a little water or milk and 1 tsp salt)

2 tbsp fresh sage, chopped

In a heavy-bottomed stock pot, fry pancetta or bacon in olive oil over medium heat until it just starts to colour. Add boar, sausage and salt and cook, while stirring to prevent clumps, until meat is brown. Add onion, celery, and carrots. Stir and cook for an additional 10 minutes. Add tomato paste, stir and cook for 5 minutes. Add milk and allow to almost completely evaporate while stirring occasionally. Add wine and stock. Simmer over medium-low heat, stirring occasionally, for an hour. Mix in puréed chicken livers and sage and cook for an additional 10 minutes.

Serve over your favourite pasta.

Oxley Estate Winery

533 County Road 50, Harrow
(519) 738-3265
oxleyestatewinery.com

WITH THEIR FIRST grapes planted in 2010, Oxley Estate Winery belongs to the newest crop of wineries in Essex County. Like many of their neighbours, owners Ann and Murray Wilson have built a lovely retail store and event centre on site.

But unlike most of their competitors, this isn't a brand new building. Despite the fact that it looks strikingly fresh, the heart of Oxley Estate Winery is a large barn that dates to the 1920s, lovingly renovated with new cedar planks. Modern and rustic at the same time, it's an incredible example of adaptive re-use of a historic structure.

It's one of my favourite buildings in the region. But if pleasing architecture and great wine isn't enough, another reason to love the barn at Oxley Estate is that it is home to a fantastic restaurant, run by chef Aaron Lynn.

While most chefs worth their salt are committed to being closely connected to the produce and meat they use, Aaron takes that passion to the next level: he's an avid angler, hunter and forager. As a result, you'll find items such as ramps, fiddleheads and mushrooms incorporated into the food he serves. While regulations forbid him from serving the animals he hunts, game meats such as duck and venison are regularly on the menu as well. One of the most popular items at Oxley are the sticky pickled duck wings, a recipe which Aaron was kind enough to share for this book. On a recently visit during dinner service, I lost track of the number of times a plate of the visually appealing dish came out of the kitchen. Everybody was ordering them.

What makes Oxley an Essex County gem is the combination of impeccable service, a relaxed but well-designed atmosphere, and approachable, local food. The attention and importance paid to the burgers and fried perch, for example, is just as high as it is for the risotto and chicken supreme.

When I asked about his inspiration, Aaron immediately—and not surprisingly—points to his time spent in northern hunting cabins. Judging by the experience I've had at the winery, it sounds like a place any of us would be lucky to visit.

Sticky Pickled Duck Wings

YIELD: 4 SERVINGS

1 tbsp ground black pepper

3 tbsp kosher salt

3 tbsp brown sugar

1 tbsp garlic powder

1 tbsp onion powder

2 tbsp ground coriander

1 bunch fresh thyme (chopped)

2 tbsp Korean chili powder

4 lbs duck wings (tips removed)

2 cups rice wine vinegar

2 cups red wine vinegar

1 cup Oxley Rosé Wine

1 red onion (sliced)

8 garlic cloves (sliced)

6 bay leaves

3 tbsp black peppercorns

6 cups grapeseed or other
neutral oil

2-4 cups cornstarch

salt and pepper (to taste)

1 cup honey

1 cup hot sauce

1 bunch cilantro (chopped)

3 radishes (julienned)

2 green onions (chopped)

3 tbsp toasted sesame seeds

2 jalapeños (sliced)

2 limes

Combine pepper, salt, brown sugar, garlic powder, onion powder, coriander, thyme, and chili powder. Rub all of the duck wings generously with spice mixture, place in a dish, cover, and refrigerate overnight.

Combine rice wine vinegar, red wine vinegar, Oxley Rosé wine, onion, garlic, bay leaves, and peppercorns in large pot. Place the wings in liquid, bring to boil, reduce heat to low, and cover. Simmer the wings for approximately 1 hour, until tender. Remove from heat, cool, and refrigerate overnight.

Place grapeseed oil in a heavy-bottomed pot or a Dutch oven, heat to 350 degrees. Remove wings from liquid, and dredge in cornstarch, shaking off any excess. Working in batches, fry the wings until they are crispy, approximately 2 minutes.

Remove from the fryer, toss with salt, black pepper, honey, and hot sauce. Garnish with chopped cilantro, radish, green onions, sesame seeds, and jalapeños. Add lime wedges on the side.

Crisp-Skinned Trout with Fennel Risotto, Green Beans and Pickled Blueberries

YIELD: 9 SQUARES

Pickled Blueberries:
1 litre fresh blueberries (washed)
1 1/2 cups sherry vinegar
2 cups Oxley Cab Franc
1/4 cup sugar
1 whole cinammon stick
1 tsp black peppercorns
1 small piece of ginger (sliced)
2 whole star anise
1 tsp kosher salt

Green Beans:
1 bunch green beans (trimmed)
1 splash sherry vinegar
1 tbsp cold pressed canola oil
salt and pepper (to taste)

Fennel Risotto:
4 cups vegetable stock
4 tbsp butter
1 cup arborio rice
1 cup fennel (finely diced)
1/2 cup Oxley Riesling
salt and white pepper (to taste)
1 lemon (zest and juice)
1 tsp chopped fresh tarragon
Fennel fronds

Crisp-Skinned Trout:
4 6 oz pieces of steelhead trout, cleaned, pin
  bones removed
salt and white pepper (to taste)
1 tsp grapeseed oil
2 tbsp unsalted butter
1/2 lemon

Pickled Blueberries:

Place blueberries in a large mason jar. Combine sherry vinegar, wine, sugar, cinnamon stick, peppercorns, ginger, star anise, and salt in a saucepot, bring to a boil, reduce heat and simmer for 5 minutes. Pour over blueberries. Cool, cover, and place in the refrigerator overnight before using them. Can be prepared a week in advance for best flavour.

Green Beans:

Fill a large saucepot with water. Add a generous amount of salt and bring it to a boil. Drop the beans into the water and cook for a minute or two. Remove them with a large slotted spoon and drop them into iced water until completely cool. Remove from the water and pat dry. Season with salt, pepper, and vinegar.

Fennel Risotto:

Heat your vegetable stock and reduce heat to low. In a large saucepot, melt butter over medium heat. Add fennel, stirring occasionally, and allow to soften. Add a pinch of salt.

Add rice, stirring constantly for a few minutes, until it is lightly toasted. Add the wine, stirring constantly, and cook until it is nearly evaporated. Add ½ cup vegetable stock to the rice while continuing to stir, until nearly evaporated. Repeat this process, tasting the rice for texture, until cooked through.

Adjust seasoning with salt, pepper, lemon juice and zest to taste. Stir in chopped tarragon.

Trout:

Pat the trout dry with paper towel and season generously with salt and white pepper. Heat a nonstick pan over medium-high heat, add 1 teaspoon oil. Gently lay trout into the pan, skin side down. Allow to cook untouched until the skin crisps. Once the fish has coloured ⅔ of the way through, add butter, and tilt the pan slightly to the side, and baste the fish with the butter for about 30 seconds. Remove the pan from the heat, squeeze the lemon over the fish, and carefully turn the fish over in the pan. Immediately remove the fish, and place it on top of your risotto, next to your vegetables, and garnish with fennel fronds and pickled blueberries.

Pause Café

74 Chatham Street West, Windsor
(519) 255-7288
facebook.com/pausecafewindsor/

It was the search for lavender ice cream that first brought me to Pause Café. I first encountered this particular flavour during our honeymoon in Portland, Oregon—and I hadn't seen it anywhere since. Somebody told me I may have some luck at a little place on Chatham Street, so I decided to check it out.

So close.

Turns out at one point Pause Café had indeed offered a lavender ice cream; but, alas, it wasn't on the current rotation. But my disappointment was brief; a look at the available flavours gave me plenty to get excited about.

Aztec chocolate with a housemade blend of chilis. Watermelon with black pepper. Rum raisin—made with real rum. Strawberry, using only fresh, in-season Essex County berries.

Twenty-five flavours are offered at the peak of summer. Each one is made three litres at a time, completely from scratch. And I don't just mean simply combining the ingredients in-house. Owner Ryan Smith—a former DJ—goes so far as to scrape his own vanilla pods.

The ice cream, alas, is only a seasonal offering. But there's an equally compelling reason to visit Pause in the dead of winter: this place makes some of the best soup in the city. Every day, a number of soups, from vegan to meaty, creamy to clear, are available. Selling both popular staples and exotic concoctions, Pause Café never fails to have a soup to match my cravings. Even better, they're available all year round.

Part of what makes Pause Café's soup so wonderful is the depth of Ryan's recipe collection. Before opening the café in March 2006, he took an entire year to find and perfect recipes that you simply couldn't find anywhere else in Windsor.

This was more than an extensive Google search. Ryan scoured dusty libraries, pouring over historic cookbooks. Harnessing the incredible diversity of this city, he spent time with a dozen of his friends' grandmothers, asking them to teach him how to cook. The result is a French-influenced café that combines techniques and flavours from around the world.

This is harder than it sounds. In my experience, many places that try to serve a taste of the world end up producing food that iswatered down or ill-conceived. Pause Café, on the other hand, sticks to the classic café trifecta of sandwiches, soups and salads, and integrates the flavours of the world into these silos. It's a good strategy.

It's clear that Ryan puts a lot of thought into the food he serves—and his dedicated cadre of downtown students and workers is proof that he has a good thing going.

While Ryan wasn't quite willing to share the secret behind his incredible ice cream, I managed to coax him to share some of his fantastic soups.

Simple Vegetable Soup

YIELD: 8-10 SERVINGS

1/4 cup olive oil

4 medium onions (diced)

5 stalks celery (diced)

2 large carrots (diced)

2 cloves garlic (chopped)

1 bay leaf

4 large tomatoes (diced)

4 potatoes or sweet potatoes (chopped)

2 cups vegetables (peas, corn, green beans, broccoli, or spinach)

1 tsp dried thyme

20 cups vegetable, chicken, or beef broth

1 tsp chili flakes

1/2 cup fresh parsley (chopped)

salt and pepper to taste

Heat oil and sauté onion, celery, and carrots over medium heat for approximately 10 minutes. Add garlic and cook for an additional minute. Add bay leaf and tomatoes, cook 5 minutes. Add potatoes, assorted vegetables, thyme, and broth. Bring to a boil, lower heat to medium and cook until potatoes are tender.

Stir in chili flakes and parsley. Season with salt and pepper to taste.

Coconut Curry Soup

1 package rice vermicelli noodles
1 tbsp vegetable oil
1 onion (diced)
2 carrots (sliced)
1 green pepper (diced)
2 cloves garlic (chopped)
1 tbsp fresh ginger (finely chopped)
10 mushrooms (sliced)
4 tbsp curry powder
1 bay leaf
1 tbsp lemon juice
1 lb tofu (cut into 1-inch cubes)
8 cups vegetable broth
1 19 oz can coconut milk
1/4 cup fresh cilantro (chopped)
1 cup bean sprouts
4 hot peppers
1 lime (cut into 4 wedges)

Boil water, add vermicelli and cook until soft, about 2 minutes. Drain.

Over medium-high heat, sauté onions and carrots in oil until soft, approximately 20 minutes. Add peppers, cook 5 minutes. Add garlic and ginger, cook 2 minutes. Add mushrooms, cook 5 minutes. Add curry powder and bay leaf, cook 2 minutes. Add lemon juice, tofu, and vegetable broth, bring to a boil and simmer for 10 minutes. Add coconut milk and cilantro, simmer an additional 5 minutes.

Ladle soup over rice noodles and top with fresh cilantro, black pepper, bean sprouts, hot peppers, and fresh-

Cream of Potato Soup

YIELD: 4 SERVINGS

1 cup butter

4 medium onions (diced)

4 large carrots (diced)

5 stalks celery (diced)

4 cups vegetable or chicken broth

8 potatoes (diced)

4 cups milk (warmed)

1/2 cup cheddar cheese (shredded)

1/4 cup fresh parsley (chopped)

6 slices bacon (cooked and chopped)

4 green onions (sliced)

Melt butter over medium-heat and sauté onions, carrots, and celery, for approximately 10 minutes. Add broth and potatoes, bring to a boil. Cook over medium heat until potatoes are very soft. Mash potatoes in pot. Add milk, cheddar and parsley.

Serve topped with bacon and green onions.

Remo's Brick Oven Pizza
2175 Parent Ave, Windsor (Caboto Club)
(519) 252-3878
cabotoclub.com

WHEN I GET a craving for pizza, it's usually for a Windsor-style pie, with its decidedly North American approach to toppings, size and cheese. But every once in awhile, I want something individual, Italian and thin-crust.

For that, I head to Remo's Brick Oven Pizza.

Located deep in the basement of the massive Giovanni Caboto Club, finding this pizzeria is almost an adventure on its own. As far as I've seen, there are no signs pointing to "pizza" or "restaurant" anywhere. My first visit to Remo's became an accidental self-guided tour of the storied Italian club, until I finally wandered into the member's bar, which, despite the name, is open to the public. Tucked away at one side of the room is a small kitchen dominated by a wood-fired, terracotta oven churning out the best thin-crust pizza in the city.

I like to call it the worst-kept secret in Windsor. Open since 2003, everybody in the city seems to know about it—I was told about the place within days of my arrival—but if you're just visiting, it's not readily apparent.

The man behind the oven is Remo Tortola. Born in Italy, Remo moved to Canada after a trip to Windsor to visit a friend. Growing up in the food business—his family owned a restaurant—Remo himself owned a pizzeria for a number of years in Italy, so opening up shop in Windsor seemed like the logical thing to do.

But it definitely wasn't going to be Windsor-style.

A pizza purist, Remo went so far as to import his oven from Europe. Many ingredients are also imported, though some local items, such as mozzarella (produced in Windsor by Galati Cheese) and tomatoes (Leamington, of course) are also used.

Over 30 different pizzas are offered. Some are classics, such as *margherita* (basil and mozzarella) and *quattro stagioni* (ham, artichokes, black olives and fresh mushrooms). Others are named after regions of Italy, like *Abruzzese* (zucchini, thin potato slices and rosemary).

Then there are the pizzas with a story, such as Al (fresh mushrooms, blue cheese, fontina cheese and capicollo), named after a friend, and George (sweet red peppers, onions, fontina cheese and blue cheese), named after Remo's dentist. There's even a Mr. Harper, which was added to the menu after a visit from the former Prime Minister. (Turns out he was a meat lover, ordering ham, Italian sausage, and pepperoni salami.)

Aside from the slightly hidden aspect of the place, what I really enjoy about Remo's Brick Oven Pizza is the fact that this is an establishment where the customer isn't *always* right. Remo has strict rules about toppings—if you decide to build your own, you will never be allowed to select more than four. He'll even come to your table and explain that when it comes to pizza, simplicity is the best policy.

That sort of thing takes guts, especially for a small business owner. I admire it greatly.

Pizza Dough

YIELD: 2 PIZZAS

1 cup water
3 cups flour
1/3 tsp dry yeast
1/4 tsp sugar (or 1 gram of malt)
1 3/4 tsp salt
3/4 tbsp extra virgin olive oil

Put water, yeast, sugar, and 2 cups flour in an upright mixer and blend until water is absorbed into the flour. Add salt and ½ cup flour, mix until incorporated.

Add the oil and remaining flour. Mix until the dough is silky and easily detached from the bowl. Put dough on a lightly floured surface and let rest, covered, for 30 minutes.

Form into two balls. Put on a tray and refrigerate for 24 hours.

Pizza Sauce

YIELD: 2 PIZZAS

3-4 medium tomatoes
2 tbsp extra virgin olive oil
a bunch of basil
2 tsp oregano
2 tbsp parmesan cheese

Clean tomatoes, remove stems and chop. In an upright mixer or blender, blend tomatoes to a paste. Add extra virgin olive oil, basil, oregano, and parmesan. Mix well.

This sauce does not need to be cooked.

Francesco

YIELD: 1 PIZZA

1 pizza dough
1 tbsp olive oil
1/2 cup mozzarella
1 roasted sweet potato (sliced)
1 tsp fresh garlic
1/4 cup goat cheese
1/2 bunch parsley

Rub dough with olive oil. Top with mozzarella, sweet potato, garlic, crumbled goat cheese, and parsley. Bake at 450 degrees until crust turns golden, approximately 10–15 minutes.

Molisana

YIELD: 1 PIZZA

1 pizza dough
1 tbsp olive oil
1/2 cup mozzarella
2 porcini mushrooms (sliced)
1/2 Italian sausage (sliced)
1 black truffle (diced)

Rub dough with olive oil. Top with mozzarella, mushrooms, sausage, and truffle. Bake at 450 degrees until crust turns golden, approximately 10–15 minutes.

Crostone Ripieno

YIELD: 1 PIZZA

1 pizza dough
1/2 cup pizza sauce
1/4 cup ricotta
1 handful spinach
1/2 bunch basil (chopped)
1/2 cup mozzarella
1/2 cup prosciutto crudo (diced)
1 tbsp olive oil

Spread sauce evenly over dough. top with ricotta, spinach, basil, mozzarella and prosciutto.

Fold dough over in half and seal edges.

Brush with olive oil and bake at 450 degrees until crust turns golden, approximately 10–15 minutes.

Rino's Kitchen & Ale House

131 Elliott Street West, Windsor
(519) 962-8843
rinoskitchen.com

IF YOU WANTED to feed someone the best of Windsor and Essex County and you had only one meal to do it, chances are you would end up at Rino's Kitchen. Chef Rino Bortolin, after all, quite literally wrote the book on "cooking local in Windsor and Essex County."

Today, many restaurants tout the fact that they use local ingredients—it's almost a given. Rino's, however, takes it to a new level. They're relentlessly local.

What makes Rino's Kitchen different is that it is more than a restaurant—it's a storefront and community hub for all things Windsor-Essex. They host local musicians, cooking demonstrations and even artisan markets. One of the most memorable events I attended at Rino's involved local butcher Jamie Waldron showing how to properly butcher one of Harold Wagner's fantastic Berkshire pigs. This isn't a large place, so it wasn't like Jamie was working on a stage, removed from the audience. He was right in the centre of the tiny dining room, while the rest of us—including the man who raised the pig!—hovered around.

A farmer, butcher, chef and customers in the same room is not something you see in every restaurant.

Rino's has also become a bit of an incubator for other businesses—food and otherwise. I first met The Blind Owl's Mark Dutka (see pages 34–39) when he started curing and aging his meats in the temperature controlled second floor of the restaurant. Today, it's home to a vintage clothing shop.

But some significant changes have occurred since the publication of the now-iconic *Rino's Kitchen* cookbook in 2013.

In 2014, Rino added city councillor to his list of titles. He represents ward 3, which runs from downtown Windsor south to Jackson Park, and includes the midtown area where the restaurant is located.

A year later, Rino sold the restaurant to Josh Fraser, his sous chef. So while the name hasn't changed, the restaurant is more accurately Josh's Kitchen, with Rino playing the role of consultant.

You couldn't ask for a better person to take over the reins. Josh has worked at Rino's since the very beginning—in fact, he was the first person hired to work in the kitchen. Just like Rino, Josh has a relentless passion for all things local, sourcing his ingredients from multiple farmers and local businesses. This conscious decision to forgo sourcing from a single food distributor isn't one that can be made easily. It undoubtedly takes longer—but the payoff is worth it.

While many of Rino's classics remain on the menu—including those fantastic pulled pork waffles—Josh has also added his own creations inspired by the bounty of Windsor-Essex, including the recipes shared for this book.

131

Jalapeño, Bacon & Cheddar Gnocchi

YIELD: 4-6 SERVINGS

1 cup chopped cooked bacon
1/2 cup jalapeño (minced)
2 tbsp garlic (chopped)
1 tbsp olive oil
2 tbsp unsalted butter
2 tbsp flour
2 cups heavy cream
1 cup shredded cheddar
salt and pepper to taste
4 cups gnocchi
chives for garnish (optional)

Cook bacon, jalapeño, and garlic with olive oil over medium heat until garlic starts to turn golden. Add butter and, once it melts, flour. Let cook for 30 seconds and stir in cream. Cook, stirring occasionally, until cream bubbles, then add shredded cheddar. Make sure you really work the bottom of the pan with a wooden spoon to deglaze and lift up all that flavour. Add salt and pepper to taste.

Boil salted water in a medium pot. Add gnocchi and stir. Once gnocchi floats, cook for another minute, strain and add to sauce. Coat gnocchi well and garnish with fresh chives.

Balsamic Strawberry & Goat Cheese Bruschetta

YIELD: 4-6 SERVINGS

1 pint strawberries
1 baguette
2 tbsp sugar or honey
1/2 cup balsamic vinegar
1 cup goat cheese
1 tbsp olive oil
salt and pepper to taste

Cut strawberries, place them in a bowl and lightly coat with sugar or honey and a splash of balsamic vinegar. Set aside for at least 30 minutes to let the flavour develop.

Slice baguette at a 45-degree angle, to allow for longer pieces. Lightly toast in a pan with olive oil.

Once the bread is toasted, spread with goat cheese and top with balsamic strawberries.

Walkerville Easy Stout Chocolate Cake

YIELD: 8-12 SERVINGS

Cake:

1 cup Walkerville Easy Stout

1 cup unsalted butter

2 cups sugar

1/4 cup unsweetened cocoa powder

2 large eggs

2/3 cup sour cream

1 tbsp vanilla

2 cups all-purpose flour

2 1/2 tsp baking soda

Syrup:

1/2 cup Walkerville Easy Stout

1/2 cup unsalted butter

1/2 cup sugar

1/2 cup icing sugar

1/8 cup unsweetened cocoa powder

1/2 tbsp coarse salt

1 tsp cayenne

Garnish:

8-12 strawberries

Whipped cream

Cake:

Pre-heat oven to 350 degreees. Butter a 9-inch springform pan.

Pour stout into a large pot and place over medium heat. Add butter and cook until melted. Remove from heat and whisk in sugar and cocoa powder.

In a separate bowl beat eggs, sour cream, and vanilla until smooth. Add egg mixture to the pot and mix well. Whisk in flour and baking soda. Pour into springform pan and bake for 50 minutes to an hour.

Syrup:

Pour stout into a medium pot over medium heat. Melt butter and add the sugar, icing sugar, cocoa powder, coarse salt, and cayenne pepper. Mix well. Reduce heat and let syrup reduce for 5–10 minutes.

When the cake is finished (a cake tester such as a knife comes out clean) place on a rack to cool.

Before serving, spoon the sauce over each piece and garnish with some whipped cream and strawberries.

Robbie's Gourmet Sausage Co.

1506-1512 Wyandotte Street East, Windsor
(Entrance on Gladstone)
(519) 567-4377
facebook.com/RobbiesGourmetSausages

For years, Rob Bornais worked at a local golf course.

It wasn't in the kitchen. Rob was the second assistant superintendent, meaning he was part of the team that looked after the grounds—pesticide management, training staff, that sort of thing. At this point in his life, I'm told, he barely knew how to cook.

That all changed during a vacation to Mexico in 2004, when Rob happened to try a particularly delicious chorizo sausage—the first he'd ever had. When he got back to Windsor, Rob searched far and wide to find a chorizo like the one he'd had in Mexico. Nothing came close.

It haunted him. Eventually, he decided to take matters into his own hands.

Rob experimented. He tasted. He researched. Though he ordered some textbooks from the Culinary Institute of America, no formal classes were involved. Over the next eight years, Rob became a 100 percent self-taught, sausage-making expert.

In 2012, Rob felt ready enough to present his work to judges—so he entered the Great Canadian Sausage Making competition in Abbotsford, British Columbia. If he did well here, Rob figured, maybe a career change into the sausage-making business could be in the cards.

He won in the four categories that he entered—including chorizo. In fact, that chorizo was crowned best sausage in Canada.

I first met Robbie when he started selling his sausages at the Downtown Windsor Farmers' Market in summer of 2013. His classic sausages were fantastic—including that incredible fresh chorizo—but it was his concept of "conceptual" sausages that I fell in love with. I'm talking sausages that are a little more outside the box. Like Bacon Double Cheeseburger. Or Chicken and Ribs. Even his breakfast sausage is a little out of the ordinary, thanks to the addition of maple infused bacon, maple syrup, and sweet basil.

With a constant rotation of new offerings—some even inspired by historic sausage recipes—Rob developed a loyal clientele, myself included. I've even had the honour of being asked to participate on a couple of his tasting panels, a concept he uses when developing some of his most cutting-edge items.

In 2015, Rob opened a beautiful bricks and mortar location in Walkerville, selling not just his sausages, but goods from a number of local business, including Little Foot Foods (see pages 110–115). Small but mighty, it's a shop that makes this city grand. Rob developed these recipes in collaboration with Chef Navdeep Sehmbi from Atmosphere Fine Foods—a local caterer whose sauces Robbie has served since his farmers' market days.

Mediterranean Lamb Sausage

YIELD: 28 SAUSAGES

1 tbsp plus 1/2 tsp Windsor Kosher Salt

1 tsp coarsely cracked black pepper

1 1/2 tsp ground cayenne

1 tsp onion powder

1 tsp cumin

1 1/2 tsp coriander

1/2 tsp allspice

1/2 cup finely minced fresh cilantro (leaves and stems)

2 1/2 tsp fresh minced garlic

1 tbsp finely chopped fresh mint

2 tbsp dry red wine

2 tbsp tomato paste

1/4 cup roasted pine nuts

3 lbs lamb meat from leg

12 feet lamb casings

In a small bowl, combine salt, pepper, cayenne pepper, onion powder, cumin, coriander, and allspice. Set aside in refrigerator.

In another bowl combine cilantro, garlic, mint, red wine, tomato paste, and pine nuts. Set aside in refrigerator.

Chill lamb in freezer for 20 minutes prior to grinding. Grind twice through a ¼-inch plate.

Combine all of the ingredients with the meat and mix by hand.

Stuff into lamb casings and tie into 5-inch links.

Mussels with Chorizo and Shrimp in Wine

YIELD: 2 SERVINGS

1 lb chorizo

1/4 cup of extra virgin olive oil

1 large onion (diced)

1 large red bell pepper (diced)

1 jalapeño (halved and sliced)

1 head of garlic (minced)

3 tomatoes (diced)

salt and pepper (to taste)

1/2 tsp ancho powder

1/2 tsp Spanish paprika

2 lbs mussels (cleaned)

1 lb shrimp

1 nice loaf of crusti bread

Garnish chives, parsley, cilantro (chopped, optional)

Pre-heat oven to 425 degrees. Place chorizo on parchment paper on a cookie sheet. Cook for 15–17 minutes or until it reaches an internal temperature of 152 degrees. Remove from oven and wrap in tinfoil pouch. Refrigerate for 24 hours.

Heat a pot over medium to high heat with ¼ cup of extra virgin olive oil. Add onions and cook for 2 minutes. Add bell peppers and jalapeño and cook for an additional 2–4 minutes.

Add garlic and simmer for 1 minute. Add tomatos salt, pepper, ancho powder, and paprika, continue simmering for 1 minute.

Add mussels into pot and mix thoroughly. Add shrimp, stir once, and cover pot for 5 minutes. The mussels should be opened and the shrimp a nice pink colour. Discard any mussels that did not open.

Add salt to taste.

Ladle seafood into a nice dish and drizzle broth and sliced chorizo overtop.

Garnish with herbs and serve with fresh bread.

Apple Butter & Sage Lollipops

YIELD: 8 SERVINGS

1 lb apple butter & sage sausage
1 cup raspberry balsamic vinegar
canola oil
1 1/2 cups flour
1 1/2 tsp baking powder
pinch of salt
2 tbsp sugar
2 eggs
1 1/2 cups buttermilk
1/8 tsp vanilla extract
3 tbsp butter (melted)
vanilla ice cream
mint leaves

Pre-heat oven to 425 degrees. Remove casings from sausages. Form sausage into small meatballs. Place on cooling rack on top of a cookie sheet lined with parchment. Cook for 15–20 minutes or until internal temperature reaches 152 degrees. Cool, cover with tinfoil and refrigerate overnight.

In a medium saucepan bring raspberry balsamic vinegar to a boil. Reduce to low heat and simmer, stirring often, until reduced by half, approximately 20 minutes.

Heat canola oil in deep fryer to 350 degrees.

In large bowl, mix together flour, baking powder, salt, and sugar.

In a separate bowl, whisk together eggs and buttermilk. Then whisk liquid mixture into dry ingredients until combined. Stir in melted butter and vanilla. Set aside in fridge.

Once the fryer is heated, dip the sausage balls into the cold waffle batter and slowly drop them in the fryer one at a time. Cook for 5 minutes or until golden brown. Remove and drain on paper towels. Serve on scoop of vanilla ice cream. Drizzle with raspberry balsamic reduction and garnish with mint leaf.

Snackbar-B-Q
39 Chatham Street East, Windsor
(519) 977-6227
snackbarbq.ca

The Willistead
1840 Wyandotte Street East, Windsor
(519) 253-8226
thewillistead.com

OFFERING GOOD FOOD in a well-designed space is easier said than done. Many restaurants succeed in one or the other; but combining the two takes a certain talent. Mark Boscariol and Jim Renaud, owners of the Snackbar-B-Q and The Willistead, are talented men.

"Think of it as a movie, where I'm the producer and Jim is the director," explains Mark, when I asked him how they run their empire. Jim, a chef with 30 years experience in kitchens all over Windsor and Essex County, is in charge of the food. Mark is in charge of marketing and promotion. Responsibility for the front of the house—the dining rooms—is shared.

Together and separately, Mark and Jim have been the driving force behind nearly a dozen restaurants. Snackbar-B-Q opened its doors in December 2014, and when the opportunity presented itself, they took over the reins of The Willistead—which had opened under different ownership in 2013—a few weeks later. Despite being relative newcomers, both restaurants have managed to become institutions on the local scene.

Walk into Snackbar-B-Q and you could be forgiven for wondering if there was a relationship with Slows, the legendary barbecue restaurant in Detroit's Corktown neighbourhood. Both establishments share an industrial chic décor, a pronounced commitment to craft beer and, most notably, a number of housemade barbecue sauces on the table. It's not a bad thing—if you're going to follow a formula for a successful urban barbecue restaurant, Slows is one of the best. But Snackbar-B-Q isn't a copycat.

Whereas Slows has a handful of great options for vegetarians, Snackbar-B-Q's menu goes so far as to proclaim "Vegetarians Welcome!" with items such as smoked tofu, fried green tomatoes and even buffalo cauliflower wings featuring prominently. Like Windsor itself, the food at Snackbar-B-Q is multicultural, with kimchi-stuffed steamed bao buns, jerk-fried chicken and smoked polenta sharing space with traditional American barbecue mainstays such as ribs and pulled pork.

Over at The Willistead, the idea of using animals from nose to tail drives what Jim creates, instead of a particular culinary style. You'll find items such as heart, cheek and blood sausage on the menu, which changes multiple times a week. While the use of offal and less popular cuts have been gaining popularity in restaurant kitchens for some time, what The Willistead excels in doing is preparing these items in a manner that is familiar—and therefore appealing. An example of this is the beef tongue sandwich, one of the recipes Jim was gracious enough to provide. It's essentially a corned beef sandwich that happens to use tongue instead of the more common brisket.

Kansas City Barbecue Sauce

YIELD: 8 CUPS

2 cups ketchup

2 cups tomato sauce

1 1/4 cups brown sugar

1 1/4 cups red wine vinegar

1/2 cup unsulfured molasses

4 tsp hickory-flavoured liquid
  smoke

2 tbsp butter

1/2 tsp garlic powder

1/2 tsp onion powder

1/4 tsp chili powder

1 tsp paprika

1/2 tsp celery seed

1/4 tsp ground cinnamon

1/2 tsp cayenne pepper

1 tsp salt

1 tsp coarsely ground black
  pepper

In a large saucepan over medium heat, mix together ketchup, tomato sauce, brown sugar, wine vinegar, molasses, liquid smoke, and butter. Season with garlic powder, onion powder, chili powder, paprika, celery seed, cinnamon, cayenne, salt, and pepper. Stir well.

Reduce heat to low, and simmer for up to 20 minutes. Sauce can be thinned using a bit of water if necessary.

Brush sauce onto any kind of meat during the last 10 minutes of cooking.

Alabama White Sauce

YIELD: 8 CUPS

4 cups mayonnaise
1/4 cup apple cider vinegar
3 tbsp corn syrup
1 1/2 tbsp garlic (minced)
1 tsp cayenne pepper
1 1/2 tsp prepared horseradish
1 1/2 tsp sea salt
1 tsp ground black pepper
lemon juice (to taste)

Place all ingredients in a very large blender or food processor. Blend for 1 minute, or until thoroughly combined and mixture is smooth. Pour sauce into a large bowl.

Use when grilling chicken; brush lightly over the chicken during the last few minutes of grilling. This sauce is also great for dipping.

Cauliflower Fritters

YIELD: 2 SERVINGS

2 cups cauliflower florets (cooked)
1 egg (beaten)
1/4 cup green onions (minced)
2 tbsp feta cheese
1/2 tsp onion powder
1/2 tsp garlic powder
1/2 tbsp fresh mint (chopped)
1/2 tsp baking powder

In a large mixing bowl mash fresh-cooked cauliflower. Add egg, onion, feta, onion powder, garlic powder, mint, and baking powder. Mix well and form 8 fritter patties. Coat non-stick skillet with cooking spray and cook until golden brown on each side.

Beef Tongue For Sandwiches

YIELD: 8-10 SERVINGS

Beef tongue:
1 whole beef tongue

Corned beef brine:
16 cups water
1 large onion (diced)
2 carrots (diced)
2 stalks celery
6 cloves garlic
10 allspice berries (whole)
15 peppercorns (whole)
1/2 bunch thyme
1 bunch parsley
1 cup salt
1 cup sugar

In a stainless steel pot add water, onion, carrot, celery, garlic, allspice, peppercorns, thyme, parsley, salt, and sugar. Boil for 5 minutes to infuse flavors. Remove from heat and cool completely. Put tongue in brine and refrigerate for 24 hours.

Remove tongue from brine and place into a large pot. Add half of the brine and all of the spices and vegetable from the brine. Add an equal amount of water into the pot, bring to a boil, then reduce to a simmer and cook for 6–8 hours until tender.

Remove tongue from pot and cool. Peel away the outer skin and remove bones from the end. Wrap the tongue in plastic wrap and cool overnight.

Slice medallions off of the whole cooked tongue and layer onto thick-cut bread with your favorite toppings or a smear of spicy brown mustard.

The Squirrel Cage
1 Maiden Lane West, Windsor
(519) 252-2243
thesquirrelcage.ca

THE SQUIRREL CAGE will always have a special place in my heart. It was the first building in Windsor I ever visited, and owners John Ansell and Steven Thompson were the first Windsorites I'd ever met. With its reclaimed wood tables, delicious food, location on a beautiful, pedestrian-friendly alley, and owners brimming with hope for Windsor's future, I couldn't have asked for a better introduction to the city.

The Squirrel Cage opened in July 2012, weeks before I arrived in town. Like me, John and Steven weren't from Windsor. In fact, they both had successful careers in Toronto: John was in real estate, and Steven was a stock broker.

However, both men had spent time working in cafés, and opening one of their own was a shared dream. But starting such an endeavour in Toronto was an expensive and risky proposition. Steven's mother lived in Windsor, and so the two visited the city regularly. They began to see potential—and combined with rock-bottom property values, realized that it might just be the place to open up shop. They purchased a former hair salon and massage parlour and set about to convert the bottom level into a coffee house and the top into their home. If it didn't work out, they had the type of jobs they could always return to.

Four years later, I think it's safe to say that these two are here for the long haul. The Squirrel Cage is one of the most popular cafés in Downtown Windsor. The wait for Sunday brunch can sometimes reach 45 minutes.

During the week, the place is a mainstay for office workers in the area; on the weekends, tourists take over.

Today, John and Steven are as integral to Maiden Lane as Daniel Bombardier's iconic street art. In 2015, they opened up Buuntz & Co., a seasonal ice-cream shop in the alley. This year, it was joined by A Dog's Breakfast, which specializes in burgers, hot dogs and brunch classics.

Cheesy Shrimp Dip

YIELD: 6 SERVINGS

1 tbsp butter

3 cloves garlic (minced)

1 454 gram bag of shrimp (tails removed and diced)

1 package Boursin cheese

1 medium sized brie wheel

1 tbsp fresh thyme

In a pan melt butter over medium heat. Add minced garlic and sauté for a minute or two, then add diced shrimp and cook until shrimp turns pink, approximately 2 minutes.

Transfer to oven-safe dish and add crumbled Boursin, chunks of brie, and thyme.

Pre-heat oven to 375 degrees. Cook dip for approximately 20–30 minutes until all the cheese is melted. Remove from oven, stir and serve with pieces of fresh baguette.

Smoked Salmon Quiche

Dough:
2 1/2 cups flour
1/2 tsp salt
2 tbsp butter (cubed)
1 cup shortening (cubed)
10 tbsp of ice water

Quiche:
8 eggs
1 litre half and half cream
1 tsp white pepper
1/2 tsp salt
1 pinch nutmeg
12 oz cream cheese
2 tbsp capers
1 bunch dill
8 oz smoked salmon

Mix flour and salt in an upright mixer, add butter and shortening. Continue mixing until you get an oatmeal consistency. Slowly add water 1 tbsp at a time until the dough forms a single ball on the mixer paddle. Remove and chill for 10 minutes in the fridge. Cut in half, roll out and place in 2 greased oven safe pie plates.

In a large bowl whisk eggs, cream, pepper, salt, and nutmeg. Set aside.

Place cheese in bottom of pies, add capers and dill. Lay salmon on top. Add egg mixture evenly between both pies.

Cook in oven at 425 degrees for 15 minutes then reduce to 350 degrees and bake for an additional 25 minutes. Remove from oven once no more liquid is visible.

Spicy Red Lentil Soup

YIELD: 10 SERVINGS

2 cups dry red lentils
4 cups potatoes (diced)
2 cups onion (finely chopped)
20 cloves garlic (whole)
12 cups water
2 tbsp canola oil
2 tbsp ground cumin
1 tbsp ground turmeric
1 tbsp salt
1 tbsp cayenne pepper
1 bunch cilantro (finely chopped)
6 tbsp fresh lemon juice
salt and pepper (to taste)

In a large pot, mix lentils, potatoes, onion, garlic, and water. Boil over medium-high heat, stirring often until potatoes are softened, approximately 15–20 minutes.

In a separate pan heat oil on high. Add cumin, tumeric, salt, and cayenne pepper and cook for 2 minutes. Add spice mixture to soup, stirring well. Stir in cilantro and lemon juice and simmer over low heat for approximately 1 hour. Add salt and pepper to taste.

Taloola Café

396 Devonshire Road, Windsor
(519) 254-6652
taloolacafe.com

LINDA ZAGAGLIONI IS a well-travelled woman. While the places she visited were incredibly varied, one thing stayed the same: visits to small cafés. As an artist, she loved how these spaces acted as places to indulge and gather.

"Why can't we have one of these places in Windsor?" she'd invariably ask herself.

One of the buildings she always thought would make a great café was the old Crown Inn, a gorgeous four-storey affair on Devonshire Road. Completed in 1893, it was the first hotel in Walkerville. The idea percolated for years, but she never fully pursued it.

It was a series of fortunate events which led to the opening of Taloola. A hairdresser by day, Linda joined a friend who had opened a salon in one of the ground-floor retail units of the Crown Inn. A year after opening, her friend expressed a desire to sell the salon. With an empty unit next door, Linda decided to make a move.

In March 2006, Taloola Café opened its doors. It is named after Tallulah Bankhead, an iconic early American stage and film actress.

I first visited Taloola in 2012, a few weeks after moving to Windsor. Walking in, I was transported immediately back to my student days. A small university town, downtown Peterborough has a plethora of small coffee houses in old buildings. Open late, selling fair-trade coffee, inexpensive meals with plenty of vegetarian options, and filled with comfortable chairs, I'd been visiting these places since I was a teenager.

Taloola was just like this, but with even better food and drink.

One of the first things I ordered was the "Mango Lovely" smoothie. A simple combination of yogurt, honey and mango, I was surprised by the addition of a touch of rose water. An ingredient common in the Indian desserts I ate as a child, it's a small touch that gives the drink a taste of comfort and home. Linda, who designed the menu herself, describes the food as being prepared how she would at home—everything is made from scratch, using fresh ingredients. While the café offers many items with meat, Taloola has built a well-deserved reputation for being a particularly friendly restaurant for vegetarians. In fact, all the recipes Linda has shared for this book are vegetarian.

In the space of a decade, Taloola has cemented itself as a cornerstone of life in Walkerville, drawing in people from both the neighbourhood and across the city. It's a place to take in live music, to write, and yes, to simply indulge and gather.

Taloola Smoothies

Figlioni:
1/2 cup yogurt
3 tbsp pure fig jam
1/4 cup pecans
1/2 cup ice

Blend on high until well mixed.

Mango Lovely:
1/2 cup yogurt
1/2 cup milk
1 tbsp honey
1 cup frozen mango chunks
1 tsp rose water

Blend on high until well mixed.

Vanilla Rose Cake

YIELD: 8-12 SERVINGS

Cake:
3 cups unbleached all-purpose flour
4 tsp baking powder
1/2 tsp salt
1 1/2 cups sugar
1 1/2 cups soy milk
4 tsp pure vanilla extract
1/2 cup canola oil
egg replacer (equal to 2 eggs)

Frosting
1/2 cup Earth Balance margarine
4 1/2 cups icing sugar
4 tbsp soy milk
2 tsp rose water

jar of rose jam
dried rose tea

In a large bowl, stir together flour, baking powder, and salt. Add sugar, soy milk, vanilla extract, canola oil, and egg replacer. Stir together until just mixed.

Line two 8-inch round cake pans with parchment paper and grease well. Pour batter evenly into cake pans and bake at 350 degrees for 25–30 minutes.

Cool completely before applying jam and frosting.

Blend margarine, icing sugar, soy milk, and rose water until smooth.

Spread the rose jam on the top of one of the baked cake rounds. Place the other cake on top. Frost cake and sprinkle the top with a dried rose tea of your choice for decoration.

Nice Rice

Dressing:

1 cup prepared mango chutney (we use
    Hawberry Farms Mango Chutney)

1/4 cup finely minced garlic

1/2 cup unsweetened shredded coconut

1/2 cup puréed fresh ginger

2 1/2 cups olive oil

1 1/2 cups of cooked organic brown rice

1/4 cup red cabbage (shredded)

1/4 organic carrot (shredded)

1/4 cucumber (sliced)

1/4 red pepper (sliced)

1/4 small red onion (sliced)

1/2 avocado (sliced)

1 handful organic spinach

Place mango chutney, garlic, coconut, and ginger into a food processor.

Process while slowly adding 2½ cups of good quality olive oil until mixture is smooth.

Over a bed of rice arrange cabbage, carrot, cucumber, red pepper, onion, avocado, and spinach. Sprinkle with black cumin seeds and drizzle with dressing.

Extra dressing can be stored in the refrigerator for up to 2 weeks.

Ukrainian Restaurant
1148 Marion Avenue, Windsor
(519) 253-3981

WHEN I GO out to record an interview for my radio column, one of the things I have to keep in mind is the amount of tape that I gather. Generally, my columns run 6-8 minutes long; the actual tape used from the interview is usually no more than 3-4 minutes.

As a result, I try to keep my interview no longer than 15 minutes; at most 20. Anything more becomes a huge problem within the short time frame we're afforded in morning radio.

When I came back from my interview with the energetic and talkative Anna Momcilovic, owner of the Ukrainian Restaurant, I found myself with more than an hour of tape. It caused a lot of extra work—but I didn't regret a minute of it. This woman and her restaurant are a timeless Windsor institution. The Ukrainian Restaurant is nestled in the midst of a block of modest houses on Marion Avenue, between Via Italia and Ottawa Street. In 1929, the Havriluk family opened a grocery store in the building; by 1931, it was turned into the Ukrainian Restaurant. With Windsor growing rapidly into a major industrial centre, the restaurant boomed along with it, with a sizable staff and line-ups out the door.

Today, the Ukrainian Restaurant is a one woman house—quite literally, as Anna calls the living quarters behind the kitchen home. Contrary to popular belief, Anna is not Ukrainian, nor is she related to the family that originally opened the establishment.

Born in the former Yugoslavia, Anna arrived in Windsor in 1964 armed with a degree in economics. After working at a number of Windsor's hotels and restaurants, Anna decided to get into the restaurant business herself and purchased the restaurant in 1968. Mrs. Havriluk helped Anna out for the first few months, teaching her the essentials of what made the restaurant so popular.

Even today, stepping into the restaurant is like stepping back into the 1930s; Anna tells me that beyond the addition of some pictures of herself and her family she hasn't changed the interior very much since she took over. The menu has also stayed pretty much the same, offering mainly cabbage rolls, perogies, sausages and stuffed peppers, with items such as strudel and walnut torte for dessert. Everything is made in-house, including the sauerkraut, and, of course, cash is the only method available for payment.

Anna's customers generally fall into two camps: families that have been coming to the restaurant for decades, and the "internet people," individuals who happen to stumble upon the place online.

Most—especially the "internet people"—order the perogies and cabbage rolls. I'm no exception—that's what I ordered the first time, too. But it's the stuffed peppers that Anna loves the most—and I completely understand why. Her version single-handedly made me a believer. Most restaurants serve this dish using sweet bell peppers, but Anna uses Hungarian peppers, which have a slightly thinner skin and give out some heat. In a city crazy for Eastern European comfort food, it's the small, elegant touches like this that make the Ukrainian Restaurant an enduring Windsor institution.

Stuffed Peppers

1 cup rice
5 small onions
4 cloves garlic
2 lbs ground pork
1 lb ground beef
5 eggs
3 tbsp salt
1 tbsp pepper
1 tbsp sweet paprika
1 tbsp caraway seed
8-10 large Hungarian peppers
3 cups tomato juice
3 cups water

Wash rice, then add to pot of boiling water and cook for seven minutes. Remove and strain rice, set aside.

Peel and then shred onions and garlic in processor to purée consistency.

In a large mixing bowl, add pork, beef, onion and garlic purée, eggs, rice, salt, pepper, paprika, and caraway seed. Mix to uniform consistency.

Cut insides of pepper out. Fill peppers with meat mixture.

Place peppers in a large pot, add tomato juice and water. Cook until boiling on high, reduce heat to low and cook for 1 hour.

Borscht

YIELD: 12 SERVINGS

10 cups water

2 cups tomato juice

8 medium-sized beets

2 carrots

1 parsnip

3 medium potatoes

1/2 head of cabbage

salt

6 tsp sour cream

6 tbsp 35% whipping cream

In a large pot cook water and tomato juice over high heat until it boils, then reduce to low. Peel beets, carrots, parsnips, and potatoes and shred. Shred cabbage. Add to tomato and water and cook over low heat for 45 minutes.

Add salt to taste.

Serve each bowl with 1 teaspoon sour cream and 1 table-spoon whipping cream.

Potato and Cheddar Perogies

4 cups flour

1 egg

3 tbsp plus 1 tsp salt

1 tbsp butter

1 cup warm water

5-6 medium potatoes

1 1/2 cups cheddar cheese

In a large bowl mix flour, 1 teaspoon salt, egg, and butter. Mix contents, adding warm water sparingly. Add water until dough is smooth and it reaches a pizza-dough consistency. Cover and set aside.

Peel potatoes and add to a pot of water with 3 tablespoons salt. Boil for approximately 30 minutes or until cooked through. Drain. In a mixing bowl, combine potatoes and cheese. Cool. Roll into small balls.

Roll out dough on lightly floured surface to a ⅛-to-¼-inch thickness. With the open end of a glass cut out circles in the dough. Put potato balls in center of circles, fold in half and press ends together.

Put perogies in boiling water and cook for approximately 5–10 minutes. Serve with fried onions, sour cream and fried bacon.

For crispier perogies, sear in butter or oil after boiling.

Wagner Orchards & Estate Winery

1222 Lakeshore Road 103, Lakeshore
(519) 723-4807
wagnerorchards.com

HAROLD WAGNER IS one of the most interesting farmers I've had the pleasure of meeting. An incredible entrepreneur, this man is always up to something new—and as a result, he's one of the few people I've done more than one story on for the CBC.

A lot of this has to do with the sheer diversity of his operation. The Wagner family farm may very well be one of most interesting farms in the nation.

It all started in the 1980s, when Harold, who grew up on a cattle farm north of Oakville, met his wife Janice at the University of Guelph. He was studying agriculture, she was becoming a veterinarian. After a number of stints around the province, they eventually ended up back in Windsor-Essex, where Janice is from. She established what would become a successful veterinary practice, and seeing the potential for fruit trees in the fertile Essex county soil, he planted their first apple trees on a property in Maidstone (now a part of Lakeshore) in 1986.

It wasn't meant to be a U-Pick operation—but disaster pushed Harold in that direction when the first crop was ready in 1991. A hailstorm had marred the appearance of the apples, meaning commercial buyers would only buy the apples for juice.

Juice apples don't exactly pay the bills, so Harold placed an ad in the paper inviting people to pick their own apples. Visitors would pay a cheaper price for apples than they would at the grocer, and Harold would make more than he would from a commercial buyer. It proved so popular that today a visit to Wagner's Orchard in the fall is an Essex County right of passage. In 2015, 40,000 people dropped by.

But Wagner's is so much more than picking your own apples. There's the estate winery, which produces fruit wines and the best hard cider I've ever enjoyed. There's the honey from the on-site apiary, run by his oldest son, Matthew. About 75 head of cattle and about 30 Berkshire pigs call Wagner's home, too, a nod to Harold's upbringing. You can buy the meat raw or prepared into items such as smoked pork chops and, incredibly, gourmet pepperettes.

And then there's the kitchen.

Seemingly always in a state of expansion, Harold's industrial take on a country kitchen is run by his daughter, Katrina, a professionally-trained chef. They cater events off and on site—and produce some of the best baked goods in the county. Their incredibly authentic version of mincemeat pie—featuring ground beef and pork raised on the farm—single-handedly changed my mind about a Christmas-time dish I used to hate.

Whenever I drop by Wagner's, I always make sure to ask "What's new?" The answer never disappoints me.

Wagner's Autumn Apple Pie

YIELD: 6-8 SERVINGS

Pie Dough:

2 cups pastry flour

3/4 cup baking lard or vegetable shortening

1 tsp salt

1/4 cup cold water

Filling:

4 3/4 cups peeled, cored, sliced apples

1/2 cup brown sugar

2 tbsp flour

1 tsp cinnamon

1 tbsp cream

3 1/2 tsp white sugar

Dough:

Mix flour, lard, salt, and water in upright mixer with the paddle attachment until combined, approximately 2 minutes. Divide dough in half. Roll out to an 11-inch circle about ⅛-inch thick.

Filling:

Peel, core, and slice apples. Combine with brown sugar, flour, and cinnamon until well-coated.

Place filling into buttered pie crust and crimp top on around the edges. Brush top with cream and sprinkle with white sugar. Bake at 375 degrees for 40–45 minutes or until crust is golden brown.

Wagner's Holiday Mincemeat Pie

YIELD: 6-8 SERVINGS

1/2 lb ground beef

1/2 lb ground pork

2 cups seedless raisins

2 cups dried black currants

1 1/2 cups white sugar

2/3 cups brown sugar

3/4 orange

3/4 lemon

3/4 cups citron peel or mixed peel

3 1/4 cups apples (peeled, diced)

2/3 cup apple cider

1/3 cup molasses

1 tsp ground cloves

1 1/8 tsp cinnamon

1 pie dough (recipe page 193)

3 1/2 tsp cream

1 tbsp white sugar

In a large frying pan, sauté ground beef and ground pork over medium heat until brown.

In a separate pot, combine raisins and currants, cover with water, bring to a boil, turn off stove and let sit for 10 minutes. This will rehydrate the dried fruit. Without peeling, dice lemons and oranges into small pieces. Peel and dice apples.

Strain raisins and currants and combine with lemons, oranges, apples, and citron peel. Add mixture to meat along with apple cider, molasses, cloves, and cinnamon. Simmer for 10–15 minutes.

Fill an unbaked pie crust with mincemeat and crimp top on around the edges. Brush with cream and sprinkle with sugar.

Bake at 375 degrees for 40 minutes or until crust is golden brown.

Tourtiére

YIELD: 6-8 SERVINGS

1 medium onion (diced)
1/2 lb bacon (diced)
2 lbs ground beef
2 lbs ground pork
1 tbsp salt
2 tbsp Dijon mustard
1 tbsp chopped fresh sage
1 tsp ground cloves
1 pie dough (recipe page 193)
1 tbsp cream

In a large pan, sauté diced onion and bacon over medium heat until onions are soft and translucent. Add ground beef and ground pork and cook until brown. Add salt, Dijon mustard, sage, and cloves. Mix well.

Fill unbaked pie crust with filling and crimp top on around the edges. Brush top with cream.

Bake at 375 degrees for 30 minutes or until crust is golden brown.

Local Vendors

IN ADDITION TO the places in this book, here are some of my favourite local purveyors of groceries and other food staples.

Asian Food Imports | 275 Wyandotte St W, Windsor | 519-254-5966
A great source for South Asian groceries.

Baled Food Market | 769 Wyandotte St E, Windsor | 519-253-4844
Part of the trinity of Middle Eastern grocers located on the same block of Wyandotte Street.

Bonduelle | 1192 Lacasse Blvd, Tecumseh | 519-735-2111 | *bonduelleamericas*.com
Outside of harvest season, it's nice to have frozen vegetables on hand. The fact that we can get frozen vegetables using local produce is fantastic.

Brenner Packers | 497 Cataraqui St | 519-256-4956
How many cities can say they have a source for locally-made hot dogs?

Dedas Deli | 5211 Tecumseh Rd E, Windsor | (519) 974-3332
Incredible Serbian-style butcher renowned for their ćevapčići, a mixture of different ground meats and spices that is shaped into little cylinders and grilled.

Downtown Windsor Farmers' Market | Pelissier St & Maiden Lane | *dwfm.com*
While there are many great farmers' markets in Windsor-Essex, the DWFM is the one I frequent the most. It's also this region's most successful incubator of food businesses.

Dressed By An Olive | 3863 Dougall Ave, Windsor & 366 Manning Road, Tecumseh | 519-966-1775 & 519-735-1772 | *dressedbyanolive.com*
Looking for a particular olive oil or balsamic vinegar? Look no further.

European Market | 1390 Walker Rd & 6415 Tecumseh Rd E, Windsor | 519-252-8243 & 519-915-4466 | *europeanmarket.ca*
Great place for hard-to-find European packaged goods, especially from Poland. Great meat counter, too.

Ewe Dell Family Farms | 1282 Oriole Park Dr, Woodslee | 519-723-4456
Both a farm and an abattoir, I was once taught the ins and outs of breaking down a lamb here with butcher Jamie Waldron, the author of the *Home Butchering Handbook*. You can buy cuts from the abattoir and select local butchers.

Fred's Farm Fresh International Market & Deli | 2144 Huron Church Rd, Windsor | 519-966-2241 | *fredsfarmfresh.ca*
A locally-owned supermarket with a huge selection of items sourced from southwestern Ontario's best bakeries, farms, cheesemakers and meat processors.

County Girl Garlic | 2490 County Rd 20, Harrow | countygirlgarlic@gmail.com | *countygirlgarlic.com*

Delicious local garlic that is so much better than the stuff you find at most grocery stores. You'll find anywhere from 5 to 15 varieties.

Galati Cheese Co. | 931 Tecumseh Rd W, Windsor | 519-973-7510 | *galaticheese.com*

Owned and operated by the Galati Family. It's not Windsor-style pizza without Galati-produced mozzarella. Their ricotta is an essential ingredient in my wife's lasagna, and I love to snack on their caraway seed-studded 'twist' cheese.

Gennaro Café | 1271 Erie St E, Windsor | 519-977-9613

Excellent gelato, made-on-site. Available in cups, cones and take-home packaging. I'm a fan of the pistachio flavour.

Highbury Canco | 148 Erie St S, Leamington | 519-322-1228 | *highburycorp.com*

This is the company that took over the Heinz plant in Leamington when they left town in 2014. While they no longer produce the iconic Heinz ketchup, Highbury still produces some product for Heinz, including beans and tomato juice, as well as products for other companies, such as the tomato paste that is used in French's ketchup.

Honey Bee Ham | 2885 Lauzon Pkwy & 2407 Dougall Ave, Windsor | 519-945-4267 | *honeybeehamco.com*

Local producer of spiral-cut, honey glazed hams. For many Windsorites, a must-have for large family feasts.

House of Baklava | 560 Wyandotte St E, Windsor | 519-252-0888

Fantastic baklava, and one of a few places in the region to find kanafeh, the Middle Eastern answer to the cheese danish.

Hummazing | 300 Cabana Rd E & Devonshire Mall | 519-250-4866 | *hummazing.com*

When I moved to Windsor, I marvelled at the fact that residents love hummus so much that the food court at Devonshire Mall could support a local vendor dedicated to it. You'll find a number of interesting flavours in addition to the classic.

Island Café | 680 Wyandotte St E, Windsor | 519-252-3621

Most people probably associate the place with the big shawarma painting outside, but I go here for the manakish, a sort of Lebanese pizza. Available with a variety of toppings, my favourite is the simple zaatar. Buy a few and eat them at home for breakfast.

Joseph Wesley Tea | *josephwesleytea.com*

I know they're based in Metro Detroit, but you'll find these incredible teas at a few of Windsor's cafés. Owner Joe Uhl knows more about tea than anyone I've ever met—he's even written a book on the subject, called *The Art and Craft of Tea*.

La Stella Supermarket | 948 Erie St E, Windsor | 519-255-1112
The pasta aisle alone is reason enough to visit this Erie Street institution. I'm a big fan of the butcher counter, too—especially the sausages. You'll find many of Windsor's best chefs shopping here.

Lakeside Packing Co. | 667 County Rd 50, Harrow | 519-738-2314 | *lakesidepacking.com*
One of the last picklers left in Ontario—and probably the largest of the lot. I love their bread and butter pickles and hot sauce.

Lee & Maria's Market | 692 Seacliff Dr, Kingsville | 519-733-9328 | *leeandmarias.com*
Whether you pop by the market or sign up for the home delivery program, you're bound to get some of the best of what Essex County has to offer.

Mediterranean Seafood | 980 Parent Ave, Windsor | 519-252-7027 | *mediterraneanseafood.ca*
One of the last true fishmongers in the region. An excellent place for seafood from Canada and around the world.

Ming Li Vegetables | 1015 University Ave W, Windsor | 519-258-2213
This tiny Asian grocery store is a great place to stumble upon interesting ingredients and meal ideas.

Multi Food Supermarket | 799 Crawford Ave, Windsor | 519-258-9989 | *multifoodsupermarket.com*
Located in a former Price Chopper, this massive grocery store is similar to the T&T grocery store chain in the GTA and Greater Vancouver. A mind-boggling selection of produce and packaged foods from all over the world, as well as a full-service fish counter, butcher and even a separate halal butcher.

The Mushroom Hub | 840 Erie St E, Windsor | 519-252-0042 | themushhub.com
Great Lakes Mushroom Farms is a Windsor-based distributor and marketer of Canadian mushrooms. They primarily ship to stores in the US, including Whole Foods, but recently opened a retail location, called The Mushroom Hub, on Erie Street.

Orangeline Farms | 627 County Rd 14, Leamington | 519-322-0400 | zinghealthyfoods.com
The first large-scale greenhouse I ever stepped foot in was at Orangeline Farms. Primarily a pepper producer, the family-owned operation, which sells under the brand "Zing Healthy Foods," is branching out into other crops such as runner beans and even strawberries.

New Yasmeen Bakery | 1448 Wyandotte St E, Windsor | 519-252-6334
Also known as Shorouk Bakery, New Yasmeen is part of a family business that also runs bakeries in Dearborn and Ottawa. The Windsor bakery is in charge of producing markouk, a large, thin flatbread that is shipped across the continent. It also acts as the distribution point for the thousands of pitas shipped in daily from the Dearborn operation, which end up at local shawarma shops and grocers.

Italia Bakery | 571 Erie St, Windsor | 519-252-7066
A great place to buy locally-made panettone, an Italian fruit cake that is especially popular at Christmas. I also love their sesame seed hamburger buns.

Royal Pita | 713 Wyandotte St E, Windsor | 519-253-0899
The second member of the trinity of Middle Eastern grocers on the same block of Wyandotte Street.

Remark Fresh Market | 2727 Howard Ave, Windsor | 519-972-1440 | *remarkfreshmarkets.com*
An upscale grocer that has a great selection of locally produced products. Has a sister location in London.

Ruey-Feng Trading Company | 951 Tecumseh Rd W, Windsor | 519-258-4112
Just a few doors down from Galati Cheese, the Ruey-Feng Trading Company produces some of the best tofu and soy milk anywhere, made with soy grown in Essex County and marketed under the brand "Local Tofu." Most of what they produce ends up in Michigan, but you can find it at a few grocers in Windsor and at the plant itself. I love to use their pre-fried and spiced tofu in a stir-fry.

Square Deal Market | 1231 Drouillard Rd, Windsor | 519-253-4848
Originally a full-service grocer, the Square Deal Market today sells and produces only one item: Rudy's kielbasa. It's worth the trip.

Sunshine Farms | 30043 Jane Rd, Thamesville | 519-692-4416 | *picklesplease.ca*
Some of the best asparagus I've ever had has come from this farm, which is technically in Chatham-Kent. Their zesty pickled asparagus is a treat.

Sun Parlour Honey | 238 County Rd 14, Cottam | 519-839-4000 | *sunparlorhoney.ca*
One of the largest honey producers in the province, and a staple in our kitchen.

Schinkel's Legacy | 19 McGregor Place, Chatham | 519-351-0818 | *schinkels.ca*
My favourite producer of deli meat—especially their smoked turkey breast. Made in Chatham, but widely available in Windsor-Essex.

Taylor Fish Company | 419 Erie St S, Wheatley | 519-825-7366 | *taylorfishcompany.com*
This family-run fish processor is a great place to find Lake Erie perch and pickerel.

The Butcher of Kingsville | 13 Main St W, Kingsville | 519-712-9573
Thanks to the name, probably one of the best known butchers in the region.

The Cheese Bar | 226-348-5277 | *thecheesebar.ca*
Owner Sarah Barrette sources the best cheese from across southwestern Ontario, and sells them at the various seasonal markets. She also pops up at Robbie's Gourmet Sausage Co. on Sundays.

The Holistic Guy | 1270 Fairview Blvd, Windsor | 519-819-0092 | *theholisticguy.com*
Locally-produced sauerkraut and other fermented products, including kombucha.

The Pasta House | 465 Erie St E, Windsor | 519-971-9910 | *thepastahouse.ca*
Lovely fresh pasta, made in the historic heart of Windsor's Italian community.

Raymont's Berries | 445E County Rd 14, Cottam | 519-839-5422
Fourth-generation farm family growing excellent strawberries and raspberries.

Schwab's & Primo's | 1587 Tecumseh Rd E, Windsor | 519-253-3915 | *facebook.com/schwabsprimos*
A few years ago, two of Windsor's favourite butchers joined forces in a single location.

Stiemar Bread | 2640 Ouellette Ave, Windsor | 519-966-1625 | *stiemar.com*
My favourite place in the city for doughnuts. They also make excellent hot cross buns for Lent.

Tortilla Leamington | 69 Erie St N, Leamington | 519-322-5163
There are few things better than fresh, warm corn tortillas. Tortilla Leamington is the place to get them.

Union Bakery | 4081 Tecumseh Rd E, Windsor | 519-944-4323
Union is one of the few places in southwestern Ontario that makes burek, a large, pie-shaped pastry popular in many eastern European countries. Get the classic cheese burek, which contains feta and ricotta.

UR City Supermarket | 742 Wyandotte St E, Windsor | 519-962-7893
The largest of the three Middle Eastern grocers that compete on the same block of Wyandotte Street.

Walkerville Brewery | 525 Argyle Road, Windsor | 519-254-6067 | *walkervillebrewery.com*
The largest and best known craft brewery in Windsor. I really enjoy their signature Honest Lager, as well as the Easy Stout.

Willow Tree Market | 1827 Division Rd N, Kingsville | *facebook.com/thewillowtreemarket*
Last summer, my wife worked in the archives at the Jack Miner Bird Sanctuary. She often came home with some incredible produce from Willow Tree, which is just a few minutes away.

Williams Food Equipment | 2150 Ambassador Drive, Windsor | 1-888-334-3233 | *williamsfoodequipment.com*
One of the first places I turn to for kitchen equipment. They call themselves the "The Candy Store for Cooks"—and it's totally accurate.

Index

Acknowledgements

THIS BOOK WOULD not be possible without the incredible chefs, farmers and entrepreneurs who graciously agreed to share their recipes, knowledge and expertise for this book. Thank you for making Windsor and Essex County so incredibly delicious.

Thank you to CBC Windsor—especially *Windsor Morning* producer Robin Brown, host Tony Doucette and managing editor Shawna Kelly—for encouraging and enabling me to turn my passion for food and exploration into a weekly radio column.

Biblioasis is one of the most exciting cultural enterprises in this region—and I was thrilled when they asked me to join them. To Dan Wells, Chris Andrechek and the entire team, thank you for turning the ramblings of a radio man into something worthy of print.

We all know that half the appeal of a cookbook is the pictures—and I have Mauro Chechi to thank for that. Thanks for making us all look good!

My parents, Patrick and Judy Pinto, are the people I try to emulate the most. Your love, hard work, endless encouragement, honesty and home-cooked meals made me into the person I am today. Thanks for letting me order off the regular menu when I was a kid, too.

Despite the fact that Windsor is hundreds of kilometres away from our family and friends, my wife Leslie was enthusiastic from the start about making this city our home. Writing a book can be a stressful process—thank you for your support, patience and love along the way. Marrying you was—and continues to be—the best thing to ever happen to me.

About the Author

BORN AND RAISED in Peterborough, Ontario, Jonathan Pinto moved to Windsor in 2012 to join CBC Radio's *Windsor Morning*, where—amongst other things—he is the show's food columnist. The son of Indian immigrants, Jonathan's father (a chef) and mother (an incredible cook) fostered his love of good food from a very young age. A true chowhound, Jonathan leaves no stone unturned in the pursuit of flavour, delighting in finding deliciousness in the most unusual corners of the region. Jonathan lives in Windsor with his wife, Leslie—who baked her way into his heart with a delicious carrot cake.